LIBERTARIANISM IN ONE LESSON

By David Bergland

Fifth Edition 1990

Libertarianism In One Lesson
Published by Orpheus Publications, Copyright 1984,
1986, 1989 and 1990 by David Bergland. All rights
reserved, including the right to reproduce this book,
or parts thereof, in any form, except for inclusion of
brief quotations in a review. For information or
additional copies write to:
Orpheus Publications
1773 Bahama Place
Costa Mesa, CA 92626
ISBN #0-940643-00-6

TABLE OF CONTENTS

PREFACE TO THE FIFTH EDITION

The first edition of *Libertarianism In One Lesson* was written in 1984 during my Libertarian Party presidential campaign. I wanted it to serve as an unintimidating first look into that uniquely American philosophy of freedom, which has come to be known as libertarianism, and to acquaint readers with the Libertarian Party. I hoped the appeal and usefulness of the book would transcend the 1984 elections and electoral politics in general. It appears my hopes were not entirely unrealistic.

The first and second editions were inexpensively printed in a magazine style format to reach as many readers as possible during the campaign. Thereafter, many readers urged me to publish it in a more standard "book" format, which is how it appeared in the third and fourth editions. From the first through fourth editions, the substantive content of the book changed very little. We did provide more additional reading selections to satisfy scholarly readers and an appendix of libertarian oriented organizations to assist readers who sought more involvement in libertarian movement activities. Those items have been retained and updated in this current edition.

During 1988, I was contacted by an underground publisher in Poland who wished to translate the book into Polish and publish it there. It pleased me greatly to give my permission for such an endeavor. The project was a high risk venture for the publisher as the publication of such a radically pro-freedom book in communist Poland was clearly treasonous at the time. In spite of such problems, the project was a success and the book was distributed in Poland. I like to think it played some role in the revolutionary events of 1989.

The world has changed dramatically since 1988. During 1989 and 1990, communist governments were thrown out and socialist economies collapsed across the world. The Cold War ended. Privatization and free market reforms are on the rise. Even in the erstwhile "evil empire", the Soviet Union, the Supreme Soviet is adopting a program to convert from state ownership and central planning to a market economy.

As Soviet President Mikhail Gorbachev recently stated:

"Life itself has brought us to the transition to the market. We must give back to people their natural sense of being their own master. And only a normal economy, the market, can do that."

In addition, democratic elections have installed popular governments, ending decades of despotism in many countries. It is particularly gratifying that many of these changes have taken directions advocated in earlier editions of this book. Due to these profound changes in our world, this fifth edition is also modified to take account of them.

All of the news is not good. For instance, the "war on drugs" hysteria has intensified, and our civil liberties are suffering because of it. The U.S. government refuses to end its international military meddling, currently trooping off to Saudi Arabia to protect foreign oil suppliers from their Arab neighbors, risking the lives of young American men and women and wasting American tax dollars. But, libertarian approaches to even these issues are receiving more attention and may carry the day eventually.

To the reader making an initial foray into libertarian political philosophy, I say welcome. This book is a good start on the fundamentals and some of their applications. But libertarianism is dynamic, changing, evolving, as anything in the marketplace of ideas must necessarily be. My sincere hope is that you will question every idea presented here, and every idea you have learned about political philosophy elsewhere, and thus be stimulated to investigate further.

Because I am a libertarian, my confident view is that the more free and open inquiry there is into these issues, the closer we will come to that state of affairs in which both you and I will be respected and appreciated as the unique and competent individuals we are.

David Bergland
Costa Mesa, California
October, 1990

INTRODUCTION

Many people hold mistaken notions about the American political system, political ideas and political parties. Many have heard that America has a "two-party system" and assume that the only choices are the Democratic and Republican parties. Some mistakenly believe that the Constitution limits us to only two parties. Errors such as this make it difficult for new political groups or parties to grow and compete with the old, established parties.

Another common error involves the traditional political "spectrum" of left to right, of liberal to conservative. If one's thinking is limited to left or liberal on one side and right or conservative on the other, it is difficult to deal with a political philosophy which does not fit on this limited, one dimensional spectrum.

This book provides students, teachers and others interested in political freedom an introduction to the political philosophy of libertarianism and the Libertarian Party. High school and college textbooks and courses in political science and government often lack accurate information regarding libertarianism as an alternative to political views such as liberalism, conservatism, fascism, Marxism, etc. Also, parts of such texts and courses which deal with so-called "third parties" frequently do not mention the Libertarian Party or, if they do, the information is often inaccurate.

One purpose of this book is to assist the instructor in political science who desires to supplement available course material with accurate, up-to-date information about America's third largest political party and the philosophy on which it is based.

A second and broader purpose is to make available to students some basic information about libertarianism, some relevant history about the libertarian movement, the history of the Libertarian Party and how they all fit into the modern world. For advanced students of political science, additional research will be required to deal adequately with the issues discussed briefly here. Fortunately, there is a wealth of relevant scholarship available. (See the Bibliography of Additional Suggested Reading at the end of the book.) For the person who desires only enough information to make intelligent decisions about the available political alternatives in America today, the material included in this book should suffice.

CHAPTER ONE

THE NATURE OF GOVERNMENT

Government is not an entity or thing which exists independently of the people who make it up. At any time there are a number of people in our society who constitute government. They include the President, senators, governors, judges, members of Congress, state legislators, county commissioners or supervisors, city councilmen, police officers, jailers, building inspectors, fire inspectors, library managers, street maintenance men, rubbish collectors, social workers, teachers, etc.

The important point to remember is that they are just people, like you and me.

RULES OF CONDUCT, CRIMINAL PENALTIES, ARREST AND PROSECUTION

The essence of government action is this: Some people, called legislators, make rules of conduct and attach penalties for violation of the rules. When someone breaks a rule, they send men with guns (policemen) out to round up the wrongdoer and impose the penalty. This may sound like an over-simplification, but it is not.

For example, Congress has established the rule that young men must register for the draft. Any young man who fails to register is subject to criminal penalties. He will be arrested, charged, brought to trial and sent to jail if convicted.

Congress has made tax laws requiring citizens to deliver a portion of their incomes to the government's collection agency, the Internal Revenue Service. Failure to comply will make one subject to criminal prosecution. The IRS can also seize the property of citizens who, it claims, have not paid taxes. If the citizen resists, he can be put in jail just for resisting.

Some state legislatures have passed laws which make it a crime for parents to teach their children at home rather than delivering them to state school authorities. In those states, parents who teach their children at home or in private schools not approved by state education authorities will be criminally prosecuted.

On the local level, city councils pass rules telling people what businesses they can conduct, what kind of buildings they must have for their businesses, and where they can be located. Any violation of these rules will result in men with guns being sent out to issue citations, make arrests, and otherwise proceed with criminal prosecution against the violators.

The people in government who make the rules and regulations for the rest of us are not very imaginative. Lawmaking is always the same. The

1

legislature (city council, county board of supervisors, state legislature or Congress) considers a "problem", establishes rules of conduct for people, includes a criminal penalty for failure to comply, and establishes a procedure for the arrest and prosecution of those who violate their rules. Some government programs might not appear to fit this pattern, such as Social Security, national defense, the postal service, public schools, etc. However, the method of financing these various operations discloses the basic pattern. The financing method is coercive. Tax collectors compel the citizens to deliver portions of their earnings or other property to pay the costs of providing a wide range of government "services". Anyone who does not pay the tax will be put in jail under the laws as they are written today.

When anyone says, "there ought to be a law", or "the government ought to take action", what they are saying is that legislators should make certain rules, attach penalties to them, and if people do not comply, men with guns should enforce compliance by imposing criminal penalties on anyone who has broken a rule.

SOCIAL CONTRACT OR PROTECTION RACKET?

It has been said that the people of a nation or a society have entered into some sort of "social contract." Usually this is part of an argument that people must submit to the controls of government and pay taxes as the price for living in a peaceful, orderly and secure society. But a contract requires knowing persons who voluntarily enter into an agreement to accept obligations in exchange for some benefit they expect to receive. The essence of a contract is that individuals can choose to enter it or not.

The history of the development of the state, i.e., government, shows us that these institutions arose out of conquests. One tribe or group would conquer another and exact tribute (taxes) in exchange for allowing the conquered people to live. Usually the ruling tribe would provide protection for the conquered people against other marauders. Rather than a "social contract", the relationship is more accurately described as a "protection racket".

Even if we look at the American experience, which is different in that our nation was born from a revolution against British tyranny, the relationship between American citizens today and the many levels of government here is still not a social contract. How many people do you know who voluntarily signed the United States Constitution, or the constitution of the state in which they live, or the county charter, or city charter where they reside? How many have the slightest idea what these documents say?

The reality is: *there is no social contract.* Government should be seen for what it is — a group of people who have substantial power at their disposal which they can and do use to control the rest of the citizenry in a great variety of ways.

2

The ultimate question then is, "What is the legitimate use of government power and what standards should be used to determine whether government power is being employed legitimately?" To answer this most important question, let us begin by looking at the actions of individual persons and the moral principles involved.

SELF OWNERSHIP AND SELF DEFENSE

Almost everyone agrees that it is proper and legitimate for a person to use force in self defense against an attacker. The moral principle which justifies this is the libertarian principle of self ownership. Each individual owns himself or herself. No human owns another. To "own" something means that the owner has the right to decide what to do with that thing, and other people do not. As self owners, each of us has the right to control our own lives, bodies and property acquired by honest labor or trade, or by gift. Each of us also has an obligation to respect the equal rights of others. In light of this combination of our own rights and the corresponding obligation to respect the rights of others, it would be absurd if a person whose life, body or property were threatened by another were not within his rights to defend them with all necessary force.

If I have the right to defend myself, then it is proper for other people to assist me in defending my rights when it becomes necessary. This provides the answer to the question: "What is the legitimate use of government force?"

The people in government should be considered agents of the citizens. Government should be limited to assisting the citizens in defending their rights against anyone who violates or threatens them. Therefore, laws which penalize such actions as murder, rape, robbery, theft, embezzlement, fraud, arson, kidnapping, battery, trespass or pollution (a form of trespass), are valid uses of government force because such actions involve someone violating the rights of another.

By contrast, any activity which is peaceful, voluntary and honest should not be penalized or subject to government interference. There should be no laws, for instance, which penalize people for declining to be in the military, for offering goods and services to willing consumers in the market place, or for possessing types of property which others may find objectionable.

GOVERNMENT MUST RESPECT RIGHTS OF CITIZENS

Too frequently it is assumed that when a person moves from being a private citizen to being a government employee he or she becomes some sort of super human, acquiring rights denied to ordinary people. But there are no superior nor inferior human beings where rights are concerned. The people in government have the same rights as the citizens. They have the same obligation as you and I to respect the equal rights of all people. I have the right to defend myself and I can authorize my agent, the public servant in government, to assist me in defending my rights. But, I have no authority to violate the rights of others and, therefore, I cannot authorize the person in government to do it either. Just as you and I must respect the rights of others, the people in government must carry out their legitimate functions in a way which respects the rights of the citizens and does not violate them.

In conclusion, it cannot be emphasized too strongly that the essence of government is the use of force by the people in government against the citizens. When is the use of that force legitimate? The libertarian answer is that government power must be used *only* to protect the citizens from those who would violate their rights. The presumption should always be against the use of force and, therefore, the burden should always be upon those who call for government action to justify it.

We must never fail to remind ourselves that when we call for government action, we are asking the people in government to send out the men with guns to control our fellow citizens; to take part of their earnings and property in taxes; to enforce rules of conduct against them; and to impose penalties such as fines or jail if they fail to comply with the rules.

Even the legitimate use of government force is a dangerous power. We should never call for its exercise except when it is clearly necessary to defend our rights or those of our fellow citizens.

CHAPTER TWO

THE ALTERNATIVE TO COERCIVE GOVERNMENT

There are two, and only two, ways for people to deal with one another. One way is by force; the other is by voluntary cooperation.

Government is the pervasive institution in our culture grounded in force. Here in America, from its beginnings until the middle of the 19th Century, we had another institution based on force: slavery. Even this abominable institution was backed by government power through the fugitive slave clause of the U.S. Constitution and the Fugitive Slave Acts passed by Congress.

It is clear that government is an institution based on force when we observe that government does not produce anything and the people who constitute the government receive their pay from the citizens through the coercive financing method called taxation. Further, private citizens are not given the choice to decline government services, operations or activities and shop elsewhere. Taxpayers must pay for and submit to government action even when they disagree with it.

GOVERNMENT: A SERVICE CONGLOMERATE?

Government can be thought of as a huge conglomerate of "service" businesses. Government employees provide many different services to the citizens, often in competition with service providers in the private sector. Libertarians raise the following questions: (1) Must these services be provided by government employees? (2) Must these services be paid for through coercion, by taxation? The answer to both questions is: No, not necessarily.

VOLUNTARY COOPERATION

The alternative to coercion as the basis for relationships among people is voluntary cooperation. In our society we see many examples of voluntary cooperation in institutionalized form. The largest and most widespread is commercial activity, i.e., the marketplace. People, as individuals and organized into companies, produce, buy and sell literally millions of different products and services. In the marketplace no one is forced to buy any particular thing, nor from any particular seller. No one is forced to go into any particular line of work nor to provide services or goods to any customer.

In a free market transaction each person enters it because, in his or her own judgment, the result will be beneficial. This is the key to understanding economic development and increasing productivity through free trade. Each participant in a transaction entered voluntarily, is better off according to his or her own values.

Contrast this to a transfer of property made under compulsion, when a person is forced to give up something at the point of a gun. Such a person will not likely think he is better off when this happens.

RESPECT FOR RIGHTS

When the legal/political framework in a society respects and protects the rights of the people living there, then all can freely trade in the marketplace. There would be no government intervention except where some people are violating the rights of others by such conduct as theft or fraud. The basis for productive trade relationships is respect for the rights of other people and the conduct of trade on a peaceful, voluntary and honest basis.

There are a great many other institutions in our society based on voluntary cooperation, such as: church and temple, the family, charitable institutions, medical research efforts, civic betterment organizations, private schools, etc. There are literally tens of thousands of groups and associations Americans enter into voluntarily to accomplish goals of their own choosing.

The premise underlying all of this successful activity based on voluntary cooperation is the libertarian principle of respect for the rights of all people. Most people, most of the time, operate on this libertarian principle of respect for the rights of others. Most people do not want to control others and do not want to be controlled themselves. As private citizens in our dealings with each other we almost always are peaceful and honest and expect only voluntary cooperation from our fellow citizens, not submission to force.

PRIVATE PROPERTY: SELF OWNERSHIP

The legal foundation for this libertarian approach, which protects the expectations of citizens in their dealings with each other, is the system of private property rights developed in English and American law. The most fundamental element of this private property system is the concept of self ownership; that is, each person owns himself or herself. No one owns other human beings.

When we speak of property we usually think of real estate or tangible personal property, such as automobiles, computers, money, surfboards, or whatever. In simplest terms, any person can acquire property in addition to his or her own body by working to produce it, by trading peacefully and honestly with other owners of property, or by receiving gifts. A legal

6

system which recognizes and protects the right of citizens to produce, acquire and exchange property rights is an essential requirement for peaceful and productive relationships among people. The more clearly defined private property rights are, and the more dependable the legal protection for property rights, the better able people are to plan for their own futures. Dependable and secure property rights mean less occasion for disputes to arise over who can do what with any given tract of land or item of personal property. The owner decides, and bears the responsibility and the consequences, good or bad.

The distinction between relationships based on force and those based on voluntary cooperation is extremely important. The crucial question is: who should be able to decide what you can do with your life, with your body, with your property? The libertarian answer is that each person has the right to make *all* the decisions about his or her own life, body and honestly acquired property. And, each person must bear responsibility for those decisions. I have no right to force others to pay for my mistakes.

Voluntary cooperation with others is never a threat to a person's right to control his or her own life, body and property. It is only the coercive mechanism of government (or the activities of habitual criminals) which constitute a threat to the rights of the citizens. Therefore, a major goal should be to confine government to its legitimate function of assisting the people in defending their rights. Only if this is done will the people have the maximum opportunity to develop the most rewarding and productive relationships based on voluntary cooperation.

CHAPTER THREE

OBSTACLES TO CLEAR THINKING ABOUT GOVERNMENT

If you listen carefully to people discussing or arguing over political issues, you will hear a number of fallacies or obstacles which get in the way of clear thinking about the issues. Following is a brief discussion of five of the most common fallacies.

THE UTOPIAN FALLACY

This is probably the fallacy most frequently encountered in political discussions. "Utopia" refers to a perfect society, a mythical place where everyone has everything they want all the time and nothing ever goes wrong. There has never been such a place and never will be on this earth. That doesn't stop the opponents of freedom from holding Utopia up as a standard. They will contend that freedom does not guarantee that everyone will be able to achieve anything they want; some will be disappointed or frustrated and there will still be murderers, thieves, rapists and other criminals. Because freedom does not guarantee Utopia, they argue, it should be rejected.

It is true: no advocate of freedom can guarantee Utopia.

So what?

No advocate of any political view can guarantee Utopia.

Utopia is not one of the options. It is simply not available. Let's be practical, examine what's available and choose the best.

There are three options in politics in America today. The first option is the status quo: government and politics as we have become accustomed to it in the last 20 or 30 years and a continuation of trends developed during those years. Most people complain a great deal about the status quo. Different people have different complaints, but the level of dissatisfaction with the status quo today is quite high.

The second option is to move toward larger government and more government involvement in more aspects of our lives with all the accompanying cost in terms of increased taxes and loss of liberty. Most Americans find that option less appealing than the status quo.

The third option is to move significantly in the direction of reducing the size of government, reducing its involvement in our personal and business affairs and reducing its costs so that we pay less taxes. The effect of such reductions would be to increase the amount of personal freedom and each person's control over his or her own life. Most Americans prefer this option to the others.

It bears repeating: Utopia is not one of the options. When you hear someone object to the idea of greater freedom by saying, for example, "but you cannot *guarantee* that all children will get a good education if we repeal compulsory school attendance laws", you are hearing the Utopian fallacy in one of its most common manifestations.

THE "PANG" (People Are No Good) PREMISE

This fallacy is found in almost every argument for government regulation or intrusion into peoples' lives. The unstated premise is that people are weak, stupid, helpless, incompetent, dishonest and dangerous to themselves and others. Consider these examples: Social Security programs are necessary because people would not otherwise provide for their own future; the draft is necessary because not enough people would be willing to defend America; drug laws are necessary because without them we would be a nation of stoned-out people incapable of doing anything; compulsory school attendance laws are necessary because parents wouldn't educate their children.

The PANG premise has a huge logical hole in it. Those who use it always exclude themselves from the class of "people" who are weak, stupid, helpless, incompetent, dishonest and dangerous to themselves and others. If the PANG premise were valid, the last thing anyone would want is a large powerful government managed by such people, running your life and mine. As one wag put it, "If people are basically good, you don't need a government; if people are basically evil, you don't dare have one."

The reality is that most people, most of the time, act properly. They don't lie, cheat, steal, rape or murder. Most of the time most of us act on the libertarian principle of respect for other human beings, recognizing that they have the right to control their own affairs, and expecting that they will deal with us peacefully and honestly as well.

THE REIFICATION FALLACY

"Reification" is a fancy word for treating a concept or a label as something that actually exists. The fallacy is in forgetting that the concept or label doesn't really exist, only people do. "Government", for instance, does not exist as a thing separate from the people who make it up. Certainly it is necessary to have a term like "government", just as we have terms like church, school, army, union, corporation, family and so on. But, none of these labels (groups) has an existence apart from and greater than the individuals in it.

Whenever you hear someone discussing what the government, or the bureaucrats, or the big corporations, or the unions did, always ask, "Which individuals did what things?" Only individuals can act and they should, of course, be responsible for their actions.

9

One purpose for engaging in this fallacy is to depersonalize people you want to mistreat. It is much easier to call for heavy taxation of "the big corporations" than to call for reducing the dividends of the pensioners, widows, and orphans who depend on pension funds which own shares in many big corporations. Another purpose is to argue that you, an individual, are less important than labels such as "society", so you should sacrifice your interests.

THE FREE LUNCH FALLACY

The most basic principle of economics has been stated: "There ain't no such thing as a free lunch." (TANSTAAFL) Although ungrammatical, the proposition is true and undisputable. Unfortunately, where political matters are concerned, many people seem to believe there is a free lunch, that they can get something for nothing.

Frequently we hear of the right to a free education, or free medical care, or that justice should be free. A look at your property tax bill or federal income tax return shows that these things are not free. Neither teachers, police, senators nor government contractors work for nothing. Government employees generally are well paid and are invariably outraged if anyone suggests they take a pay cut. And the source of payment for all government services is the earnings and property of people who are not government employees; i.e., taxpayers.

Anyone who receives some subsidy or service from government does so at the expense of other hard working Americans. The only question is whether or not people receiving those subsidies or services are the ones who pay for them, or whether they — with the assistance of government force — are able to make *others* pay.

THE FALLACY THAT LAWS WORK

Some people believe that all that is needed to make people stop doing certain things is for legislators to pass a law making such conduct a crime. (We distinguish here between criminal laws which penalize conduct which violates the rights of another, such as murder, theft, etc., and laws which penalize peaceful, honest conduct which does not violate the rights of another. Unfortunately, between one-third to one-half of our current law enforcement efforts and expenses fall into the latter category.)

The Prohibition experiment in America is instructive. During the 1920s and early 1930s, a constitutional amendment prohibited the production, sale and use of alcoholic beverages, activities which violated the rights of no one. The results were disastrous. Liquor use declined only marginally. But, Prohibition spawned organized crime. The price of the illegal booze increased, creating opportunities for tremendous profits for anyone willing to engage in the illegal activity. People of a criminal inclination benefitted most. Criminal profiteers corrupted the criminal justice system, buying off police, courts, and jailers. People lost respect for the law. Unlike a free, competitive market, smaller competitors were often disposed of by violence.

This general pattern is repeated any time a peaceful, honest activity is made a crime. People simply do not quit buying the products and services they desire just because of the risk of going to jail. The other predictable result is the creation of a "black market" which will have most, if not all, of the characteristics of the illegal market for alcohol that developed during Prohibition.

It is amusing to hear people argue that, if there were no drug laws, people would smoke marijuana or snort cocaine when the current estimates are that 25 million to 40 million Americans do so regularly. This absurdity is repeated in arguments for other laws. For instance, if we didn't have laws against immigration, thousands from Mexico and Central America would come here; or, without laws against prostitution, people would sell sexual services. These are just a few examples among thousands which daily prove that trying to suppress peaceful conduct with criminal penalties never works.

CONCLUSION

There are a great many fallacies and mistaken ideas about politics which many people believe or accept. The foregoing discussion involves five of the most commonly encountered fallacies and obstacles to clear thinking. The careful observer who stays alert to detect these fallacies, will be rewarded. In any discussion of ten minutes or more, each one is quite likely to appear more than once.

Keep this in mind. If an argument is substantially based on a fallacy, the argument is either partly or completely invalid.

CHAPTER FOUR

THE DEVELOPMENT OF LIBERTARIANISM AS AN AMERICAN POLITICAL MOVEMENT

In the year 1776, a small group of British subjects living on the eastern seaboard of the North American Continent decided to break the bonds of British tyranny. They gave notice to the world that they were doing so, and the reasons why, in the most important political document in human history, the Declaration of Independence, written by Thomas Jefferson. The opening paragraph of the Declaration of Independence states:

We hold these truths to be self-evident, that all men are created equal; that they are endowed by their Creator with certain unalienable rights; that among these rights are life, liberty, and the pursuit of happiness. That, to secure these rights, governments are instituted among men, deriving their just powers from the consent of the governed; that, whenever any form of government becomes destructive of these ends, it is the right of the people to alter or abolish it, and to institute a new government, laying its foundation on such principles, and organizing its powers in such form, as to them shall seem most likely to effect their safety and happiness. Prudence, indeed, will dictate that governments long established should not be changed for light and transient causes; and, accordingly, all experience hath shown, that mankind are more disposed to suffer, while evils are sufferable, than to right themselves by abolishing the forms to which they are accustomed. But, when a long train of abuses and usurpations, pursuing invariably the same object, evinces a design to reduce them under absolute despotism, it is their duty to throw off such governments, and to provide new guards for their future security.

The Declaration of Independence was the opening salvo in a long history of direct libertarian political action. The American Revolution has rightly been called the first libertarian revolution.

These words from the Declaration state three fundamental propositions. The first is that human beings have rights which are derived from the natural order of the universe and the nature and characteristics of human beings. Humans have a specific nature and it is the basis for the rights we have. Second, the institution of government is something created by mankind to protect these rights. Thus, rights do not come from government; people with rights create governments as a mechanism to help protect those rights. The third proposition is that when government fails as a protector of rights, people have not only the right, but the duty, to change or abolish it.

NATURAL RIGHTS

Libertarianism is grounded in what has been called the "natural rights" tradition in western culture. The signers of the Declaration of Independence were well educated, familiar with and strongly influenced by this natural rights tradition. One major contributor to their thinking and to the mainstream of libertarian thought was John Locke. Locke's major contribution was in the area of property rights. He elaborated the concept of "homesteading" as the basis for acquiring property rights. As men go out into nature as yet unclaimed, in order to establish a just claim of ownership over any portion of it, one would have to "mix his labor with the land." The obvious example would be to clear land of stones and brush for farming. Once acquired, property was subject to the control of the owner who could use it for his own purposes and, most importantly, exclude others from it. The institution of private property continues to be a central concept in the libertarian political philosophy.

CONSTITUTION AND BILL OF RIGHTS

After the successful completion of the Revolution, the thirteen new states in North America created a level of government separate from their state governments, establishing it in a document called the Articles of Confederation. Subsequently, the state governments replaced the Articles of Confederation with the Constitution, the charter for the United States government today.

The people were justifiably concerned about the creation of a potentially powerful national government which might be a source of new tyranny. Consequently, as a condition to ratification of the Constitution, the first Ten Amendments, called the Bill of Rights, were added. The Constitution created a national government with certain specified and limited powers. The framers, and the people, knew that governments have a tendency to grow and become more powerful and tyrannical. The Bill of Rights was to guard against future encroachments on the citizens' rights by the national government.

The language of the Bill of Rights shows how concerned the framers were that the new national government not interfere in the areas of peoples' lives which were precious and sacred to them.

Article One: Congress shall make no law respecting an establishment of religion, or prohibiting the free exercise thereof; or abridging the freedom of speech, or of the press; or the right of the people peaceably to assemble, and to petition the government for a redress of grievances.

Article Two: A well-regulated militia being necessary to the security of a free State, the right of the people to keep and bear arms shall not be infringed.

Article Three: No soldier shall, in time of peace be quartered in any house, without the consent of the owner, nor in time of war but in a manner to be prescribed by law.

Article Four: The right of the people to be secure in their persons, houses, papers, and effects, against unreasonable searches and seizures, shall not be violated, and no warrants shall issue, but upon probable cause, supported by oath or affirmation, and particularly describing the place to be searched and the person or things to be seized.

Article Five: No person shall be held to answer for a capital, or otherwise infamous crime, unless on a presentment or indictment of a Grand Jury, except in cases arising in the land or naval forces, or in the militia, when in actual service in time of war or public danger; nor shall any person be subject for the same offense to be twice put in jeopardy of life or limb; nor shall be compelled in any criminal case to be a witness against himself, nor be deprived of life, liberty, or property, without due process of law; nor shall private property be taken for public use, without just compensation.

Article Six: In all criminal prosecutions the accused shall enjoy the right to a speedy and public trial, by an impartial jury of the State and district wherein the crime shall have been committed, which district shall have been previously ascertained by law, and to be informed of the nature and cause of the accusation; to be confronted with the witness against him; to have compulsory process for obtaining witnesses in his favor, and to have the assistance of counsel for his defense.

Article Seven: In suits at common law, where the value in controversy shall exceed twenty dollars, the right of trial by jury shall be preserved, and no fact tried by a jury shall be otherwise reexamined in any court of the United States, than according to the rules of the common law.

Article Eight: Excessive bail shall not be required, nor excessive fines imposed, nor cruel and unusual punishments inflicted.

Article Nine: The enumeration in the Constitution of certain rights shall not be construed to deny or disparage others retained by the people.

Article Ten: The powers not delegated to the United States by the Constitution, nor prohibited by it to the States, are reserved to the States respectively or to the people.

The purpose of the Ninth and Tenth Amendments is to emphasize the principle that the United States government has no powers except those expressly set forth in the body of the Constitution. Unfortunately, in the two centuries since the adoption of the Constitution, decisions of the United States Supreme Court have essentially rejected, indeed reversed, this important constitutional principle. Today, one must find a specific limitation on government stated in the Bill of Rights to prevent federal or state encroachment.

ANTI-SLAVERY AND FREE TRADE MOVEMENTS

During the first half of the 19th Century, the most significant libertarian political activism was the abolitionist movement, aimed at eradicating slavery. The one government policy during the 19th Century most in accord with libertarian views was the foreign policy of non-intervention. As Jefferson stated it: "Peace, commerce and honest friendship with all nations, entangling alliances with none." From the administration of Washington to that of President Monroe, the U.S. policy was non-intervention in the affairs of other countries, no military alliances and free international trade. This beneficial policy was partially rejected with the establishment of the Monroe Doctrine which stated that the United States would not allow interference by European powers in the Western Hemisphere. Unfortunately, by the end of the 19th Century the U.S. government was intervening militarily in Central America and the Pacific.

A major element in the development of the libertarian philosophical movement is the science of economics. Adam Smith and his book, *Wealth of Nations*, published in 1776, are usually credited with the beginning of modern economics based on an understanding of markets, prices, production and so forth. There were a number of other writers and economic theorists, but Smith's work was most widely known in the English speaking world.

During the first half of the 19th Century economists who advocated free markets — and especially the elimination of trade barriers between nations — were in the ascendancy. Parliamentary leaders such as Richard Cobden and John Bright in England led the movement for free international trade and demolished for all time the arguments for protectionist trade barriers.

Free trade was, and still is, a powerful inducement to peaceful relationships between countries. Indeed, it was shown that government interference with free international trade was likely to lead to war. As the French economist Frederic Bastiat put it: "If goods are not allowed to cross international borders, soldiers will."

FREE MARKET ECONOMICS: THE "AUSTRIAN" SCHOOL

The rise of Marxism in the late nineteenth century and thereafter was a powerful counterforce to libertarianism, especially in economics. Even so, libertarian theoretical work and scholarship continued. Most important was the development of the "Austrian" school of economics which, on every issue, demonstrated the need to ground economic theory in the acting individual. The logical result is that the acting individuals must be free for economic prosperity to result. The political implications of that insight are obvious.

Clearly the most significant figure in the 20th Century in Austrian economics was Ludwig von Mises. During the 1920s, Mises published one of his many important works, *Socialism*, in which he demonstrated the impossibility of economic calculation in a socialist economy. Mises showed that any centrally planned or managed economy could do nothing but flounder continually. Without a free market for goods and services, there is no market pricing mechanism to tell producers and entrepreneurs what consumers desire most. (Although Mises was ignored by mainstream economists and politicians for decades, he has been proven correct by socialism's disastrous consequences in Eastern Europe and the Soviet Union.)

DEPRESSION AND WORLD WAR II

The influence of libertarian thought in American politics was perhaps at its lowest during the 1930s depression and the 1940s war period. One great myth of American political history is that the collapse of the stock market and the following depression was the result of capitalism's failure. The historical evidence clearly contradicts this. The U.S. government's inflationary monetary policies during the 1920s and other U.S. government actions, such as stealing the gold of the people and creating substantial obstacles to international trade, simply delayed the economic corrections that would have occurred if the government had not intervened in the economy.

As Randolph Bourne wrote: "War is the health of the state." During World War II, as in all wars, the U.S. government grew dramatically in size. Controls over personal and economic activities increased as Americans were mobilized for war. Libertarian ideals of individual rights, government respect for the rights of people, due process, free markets and non-intervention in foreign wars were swept aside. Libertarian voices were among the few raised to defend the rights of Americans of Japanese descent who were incarcerated and had their property taken without due process or concern for their right to be presumed innocent until proven guilty.

POST W.W. II: ECONOMISTS AND AYN RAND

During the post Word War II period the libertarian movement in America was literally a handful of free market economists and scholars, among them economists like Mises; Henry Hazlitt; Murray Rothbard; Friedrich Hayek (later to win a Nobel Prize in economics); novelist Ayn Rand (*The Fountainhead, Atlas Shrugged*); Leonard Read, founder of the Foundation for Economic Education; and R.C. Hoiles, editor and publisher of the Freedom Newspapers.

In addition to the Austrian School of economics, a new free market oriented approach to economics was developing at the University of Chicago led by Milton Friedman, another Nobel Prize recipient. It came to be known as the "Chicago" school of economics.

The number of people who, in a knowledgeable way, came to call themselves "libertarians" during the 1940s and 1950s grew at a slow but steady pace. At that time there was no organized political movement to implement libertarian ideas in the American political arena. But in the early 1960s, a combination of factors sowed the seeds and fertilized the ground for an explicit political movement in the cause of freedom.

Ayn Rand published her major novel, *Atlas Shrugged*, in 1957. This novel sparked a movement among young intellectuals to explore further the philosophy of individualism and to challenge establishment political views. The interest in Rand was so great, that by the early 1960s, there were groups on college campuses and elsewhere throughout the country studying her novels and their philosophical implications.

VIETNAM PLUS NIXON LEADS TO YOUTH COALITION FOR FREEDOM

During the 1960s, many young people came to disagree with the U.S. government's involvement in Vietnam. Although most of the Vietnam anti-war movement leaders were from the left, some outright socialists, many activists had deeper concerns for human rights as well as the effects of the war and domestic security measures on personal liberties within America. Although libertarians were relatively few in number, they spoke out against the war, opposing the draft and opposing domestic surveillance of American citizens by the CIA and FBI.

The coalition for liberty which ultimately became the Libertarian Party developed during the 1960s and the early 1970s. Many young people came to a basically libertarian orientation by study of free market economics and by the writings of Ayn Rand. The other major group were those involved in anti-Vietnam War activity or the civil rights movement based upon a commitment to the rights of individuals to live their private lives without fear. To them, the right to engage in "alternative lifestyles" free from police harassment for their skin color, hair length, clothing styles, or living arrangements, was primary. People in both groups were not comfortable with traditional "right wing" or "left wing" labels. They finally came together at about the close of the decade of the 1960s.

Ironically, Richard Nixon was a motivating factor in the formation of a new political party which would work consistently for liberty. As the 1970s dawned, the harassment of anti-Vietnam War organizations by the U.S. government under Nixon's direction was becoming well known, certainly among those who were its objects.

LIBERTARIAN PARTY FOUNDED IN 1971

In 1971, Republican President Nixon imposed wage and price controls, demolishing any hope that Nixon or the Republican Party could be counted upon to reduce government intervention in the marketplace. As a result, a number of young people throughout the country who were committed to freedom met and decided that the American political system would benefit from a new political party which promoted freedom consistently, without exception, for everyone, on all issues, all the time. The founding convention of the Libertarian Party was called by David Nolan and held in December of 1971 in Colorado Springs. It resulted in the naming of John Hospers, head of the Philosophy Department at the University of Southern California, as the Party's first presidential candidate.

The founders of the Libertarian Party, consistent with their desire to create a political party committed to libertarian principles, adopted a Statement of Principles which has continued, virtually unchanged, since 1972. Dr. Hospers drafted the Statement of Principles, the basis for all other platform planks, which reads:

We, the members of the Libertarian Party, challenge the cult of the omnipotent state and defend the rights of the individual.

We hold that all individuals have the right to exercise sole dominion over their own lives, and have the right to live in whatever manner they choose, so long as they do not forcibly interfere with the right of others to live in whatever manner they choose.

Governments throughout history have regularly operated on the opposite principle, that the State has the right to dispose of the lives of individuals and the fruits of their labor. Even within the United States, all political parties other than our own grant to government the right to regulate the lives of individuals and seize the fruits of their labor without their consent.

We, on the contrary, deny the right of any government to do these things, and hold that where governments exist, they must not violate the rights of any individual: namely (1) the right to life — accordingly we support prohibition of the initiation of physical force against others; (2) the right to liberty of speech and action — accordingly we oppose all attempts by governments to abridge the freedom of speech and press, as well as government censorship in any form; and (3) the right to property — accordingly we oppose all government interference with private property, such as confiscation, nationalization, and eminent domain, and support the prohibition of robbery, trespass, fraud, and misrepresentation.

Since governments, when instituted, must not violate individual rights, we oppose all interference by government in the areas of voluntary and contractual relations among individuals. People should not be forced to sacrifice their lives and property for the benefit of others. They should be left free by government to deal with one another as free traders; and the resultant economic system, the only one compatible with the protection of individual rights, is the free market.

In 1972, John Hospers, the first Libertarian Party presidential candidate, was on the ballot in two states and received approximately 2,500 votes. Since that modest beginning, the Libertarian Party has become the third largest party in the country and the fastest growing.

ALTERNATIVE TO THE OLDER PARTIES

By the 1976 presidential election, the Party's presidential candidate, Roger MacBride, was placed on the ballot in 31 states and received approximately 175,000 votes. By 1980, the Libertarian Party had clearly emerged as the country's third largest party. It was the only nationwide political party other than the Democrats and Republicans with party organizations in every state.

The 1980 presidential candidate, Ed Clark, was on the ballot in all 50 states — the first time that any party's presidential candidate other than Democrat or Republican had been on 50 state ballots in U.S. history. (John Anderson, an independent candidate, was also on the ballot in 50 states in 1980.) Ed Clark received nearly a million votes in 1980, placing fourth in the balloting behind John Anderson.

In other federal, state and local elections, in all states, hundreds of Libertarian candidates have run for office, receiving millions of votes each election year. Libertarian Party activism has continued to grow steadily, particularly expanding at the state and local levels where some Libertarians are elected to office each election year.

A reaction to this growth has been stricter election laws making it more difficult for alternative parties to put their candidates on the ballot. In most states, new or smaller parties must petition for ballot position and many state legislatures have made the requirement more burdensome to discourage competition for Democrats and Republicans, who exclude themselves from those requirements. The Libertarian Party has led the fight against this discrimination with lawsuits challenging unconstitutional election laws and has lobbied Congress and state legislators for fair treatment for alternative political groups so that voters may have a wider range of choices.

The 1984 presidential election occurred at the height of Ronald Reagan's popularity. The Democratic candidate, Walter Mondale, carried only one state. David Bergland (author of this book) was the Libertarian presidential candidate. The combination of Reagan's popularity and burdensome election laws kept the 1984 Libertarian presidential ticket off 12 state ballots and the vote total low. Even so, it was the first year the Libertarian presidential candidate placed third.

In 1988, Ron Paul, a former Republican Congressman and physician from Texas, was the Libertarian presidential candidate. Still burdened by discriminatory election laws, the ticket was on the ballot in 46 states. Dr.

Paul's presidential vote total was equal to that of all other alternative parties combined. The Libertarian Party has clearly established itself as the one nationwide and effective alternative to the old political parties. One hopes that Americans will recognize the lack of substantial difference between the Democrats and Republicans and, like the people of Eastern Europe rejecting one party rule there, begin seriously considering the libertarian alternative.

Political scientists have observed that about one quarter of the population shares libertarian views. Libertarians have played major roles in projects such as Proposition 13 in California and other similar initiative and referendum efforts in many states to reduce taxes and government control of the people.

Libertarian Party candidates continue to grow in numbers, credibility and voter support. Libertarian policies such as privatization, deregulation, free trade, non-intervention in foreign wars and tolerance for alternative lifestyles are increasingly acceptable to Americans. This growth in numbers and credibility has come in spite of burdensome and unfair election laws and an apathetic press which seems disposed to protect establishment politicians from competition.

AN INFLUENTIAL INTERNATIONAL MOVEMENT

In addition to the Libertarian Party, other equally important elements of the libertarian movement are growing and becoming remarkably influential. There are a number of libertarian oriented "think tanks" or public policy institutions such as the Center for Libertarian Studies, The Mises Institute, the Institute for Humane Studies, the Reason Foundation, the CATO Institute, Citizens for a Sound Economy and The Pacific Institute for Public Policy Research. *Reason* magazine and *Liberty* magazine are influential libertarian oriented periodicals. (Indeed, it is the work done by such organizations which prepares the political ground for Libertarian Party success.) An increasing number of libertarian scholars hold teaching positions in colleges and universities and we now see judges with libertarian views on state and federal benches.

An *Appendix of Libertarian Oriented Organizations* is included at the end of this book. Many of these organizations are located, or have affiliates, in other countries. The libertarian movement is truly international. Indeed, some respected observers predict that some Eastern European countries will become more libertarian than the U.S. as they convert from socialism to radically free market economic systems. Perhaps they will serve as models for new generations of American policy makers.

CHAPTER FIVE

THE LIBERTARIAN DIFFERENCE

There are major differences between the Libertarian Party and the libertarian philosophy on one side, and establishment political parties on the other.

First, the Libertarian Party is a political organization created to implement a particular political philosophy. All Libertarian Party positions on the issues are derived from and consistent with basic libertarian principles. In capsule form, the libertarian philosophy begins with the idea of self ownership. Each person owns himself or herself. Therefore, each person has the absolute right to control his or her own life, body, speech, actions, and honestly acquired property.

Each person has these rights. Therefore, each person also has the obligation to respect the equal rights of every other person.

From this beginning point it is possible to derive a position on any political issue which is consistent with those principles. A person has the right to defend his own rights, but cannot justifiably violate another's rights when doing so. Further, no one can authorize another person to violate someone else's rights. Thus, I cannot authorize my representative in government to violate the rights of another no matter how much good I think that might accomplish. Another consequence of this obligation to respect the rights of others is that each of us is responsible for himself or herself and has no legitimate claim on the person, earnings or property of any other sovereign individual.

Contrast the Libertarian Party and its consistency to the Republican Party and the Democratic Party. It is impossible to discover the underlying philosophy of either. They have none.

MEANINGLESS POLITICAL LABELS

The label "Democrat" or "Republican" tells nothing about how a person will stand on any issue. Unlike the Libertarian Party, which has a platform that evolves from year to year without deviation from basic principles, the Democratic and Republican parties adopt a platform at each presidential nominating convention which may have little or no connection with platforms from previous years and may flatly contradict positions taken before.

While the Democratic and Republican parties have no underlying philosophical principles, they do share a basic attitude and motivation. The statements and conduct of the leadership of both the old parties manifest an elite and arrogant attitude. They have no respect for the rights of the people. They see you and me as means to their ends; as if we, our lives, our earnings, our bodies, and our property were national resources for them to exploit for any purpose they desire. By contrast, libertarians always act with respect for every person's rights and hold that people in government must carry out their legitimate functions without violating any individual's rights.

Democratic and Republican party leaders seek only to control the machinery of government, to use it to do favors for themselves and their friends. Since there is no free lunch, and since the government does not produce anything, the only way government favors can be handed out is if the resources to do so are first stolen from the remaining citizens — you and me. By contrast, libertarians seek to reduce the size and scope of government activity, confining it to assisting the citizens in defending their rights against anyone who might violate them.

Libertarians recognize that governmental favors cannot be handed out without first ripping off someone else. This is the basic reason libertarians advocate an end to the coercive method of financing government functions through taxation, and call for replacing taxation with voluntary methods of financing proper government functions.

A REPLACEMENT FOR THE MEANINGLESS LEFT-RIGHT SPECTRUM

People frequently ask: are libertarians left wing or right wing? Liberal or conservative? It is a mistake to attempt to locate libertarians on the traditional "left-right spectrum". What does that traditional spectrum measure? Nothing! And isn't it curious that political analysts and commentators rarely discuss this amazing defect in this widely used labeling scheme. Labels like "left", "right" and "moderate" are almost as useless as traditional party labels for the purpose of predicting how any particular politician will stand on a given issue.

The following chart, which is based on the analysis originally developed by Libertarian Party founder David Nolan, and further developed by Marshall Fritz of the Advocates for Self-Government, Inc., is much more useful for explaining political positions because it relates what people advocate on the issues to the relevant and important measures of personal liberty and economic liberty.

WORLD'S SMALLEST POLITICAL QUIZ
Use the Self-Government chart to see where you fit on this new political map. Begin by answering the following 10 questions. Circle **Y** when you agree, **M** for Maybe or unsure, **N** for No.

Are you a self-governor on *PERSONAL* issues?   20 10 0
1. Military service should be voluntary. (No Draft)   Y   M   N
2. Govt. should not own or control TV or the press.   Y   M   N

3. Govt. should not regulate adults' sex lives. Y M N
4. Drug laws do more harm than good. Repeal them. Y M N
5. Let peaceful people immigrate or emigrate freely. Y M N
    PERSONAL liberty score: add 20 for Y, 10 for M, 0 for N_____

Are you a self-governor on *ECONOMIC* issues?
1. Farmers should farm without quotas or subsidies. Y M N
2. People do better with free trade than with tariffs. Y M N
3. Minimum wage laws eliminate jobs. Repeal them. Y M N
4. End taxes. Pay providers for services voluntarily. Y M N
5. Europe & Japan should pay for their own defense. Y M N
    ECONOMIC liberty score: add 20 for Y, 10 for M, 0 for N_____

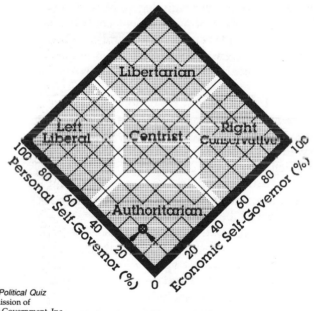

World's Smallest Political Quiz
printed with permission of
Advocates for Self-Government, Inc.

How to use the Self-Government Quiz and Map
Mark your PERSONAL score on the left and your ECONOMIC score on the right. (See example of 20% personal and 10% economic.) Then follow the grid lines until they meet at your political identity. You can also plot the political identity of politicians, public figures or groups based on how you think they would answer the questions. For instance, Margaret Thatcher would probably fall in the right quadrant, Franklin Delano Roosevelt in the left, Thomas Jefferson in the top. Stalin, Hitler, Castro, etc. are clearly at the bottom.

The Self-Government chart divides human affairs into two major areas: economic and personal. Economic matters are those which involve money, such as employment, buying and selling, investments, or business transactions. Personal matters are those which do not involve money, such as choices about what one reads, eats, drinks, smokes, wears or with whom one chooses to associate, sleep or marry. The important consideration for determining political "position" is how much (what percentage) of "self-government", i.e., liberty, in each of these two areas a person advocates. Or, conversely, what percentage of control a person wants the government to have over our personal and economic activities.

LIBERALS AND CONSERVATIVES: HOW DIFFERENT?

We can see from the chart that those customarily referred to as "liberals" advocate a relatively high degree of personal liberty but concurrently call for a good deal of government control where other people's economic activities are concerned. To liberals, we are OK in our private lives, but need to be tightly controlled when engaged in business and commerce. The typical "conservative" reverses the liberal's emphasis. Conservatives are those who advocate a relatively high level of economic freedom; that is, low taxes and reductions in government regulation of business, while concurrently calling for less personal liberty. To conservatives, we are OK while engaged in business and commercial activity, but need to be watched in our private lives lest we sin or act irresponsibly by having too much fun.

"Libertarians" are found in the upper quadrant of the chart, the location for all those who advocate a high degree of both economic liberty and personal liberty. Libertarians believe that people are OK regardless of whether they are engaging in commercial or private activities and consistently uphold the right of people to control their own lives in all respects.

The group in virtually total opposition to the libertarians are located in the lower quadrant of the chart and are referred to generically as "authoritarians." This group would include Marxists, socialists, communists, fascists, statists, populists, etc. The essential characteristic of these people is that they believe all human activity should be subject to government control and that any significant level of liberty, either personal or economic, will cause great harm.

LIBERTARIAN POSITIONS: PRINCIPLED AND CONSISTENT

Libertarianism is not some variation of left wing or liberal thinking, nor some variation of right wing or conservative thinking. Nor is it a combination of positions taken from left and right. From the chart we can see that libertarians share a common border with both liberals and conservatives. It is not unusual for liberals and libertarians to take similar

24

positions on certain personal liberties issues. Nor is it unusual for conservatives and libertarians to find themselves on the same side of certain economic issues. This is more a result of coincidence than principle. All libertarian positions on the issues are derived from the basic libertarian principles of self ownership and respect for the equal rights of others discussed earlier. The same consistent, principled approach is not true of other political groups.

Indeed, to know the position of any Democrat, Republican, liberal or conservative on any given issue at any time, you will have to ask them. They have no consistent approach for dealing with issues because they have no fundamental principles. The best you can do is compile a list of positions they hold on issues and check from time to time for any changes.

In contrast, because libertarians do have a basic set of principles, you can predict that a libertarian will always come out on the side of any issue which maximizes personal liberty and responsibility and which reduces government control over the individual citizen. The libertarian approach is to look at the people involved in any situation and ask whether or not they are dealing with each other in a peaceful, voluntary and honest way. If they are, then no one should introduce force into that situation. None of the participants should start using force on the others because that would violate someone's rights. No uninvited third party, including anyone from government, should bring force into the situation to make people act in ways they would not voluntarily act.

This does not mean that one should decline to offer assistance, help, or advice which people might accept voluntarily to deal with their problems. In fact, libertarians support the idea of offering assistance to people who have problems. But the political issue is this: when is it legitimate for the government to use force? We must continually ask ourselves that very important question. Libertarians will always answer: only to defend the rights of the citizen.

COMPARING LIBERAL, CONSERVATIVE AND LIBERTARIAN

Following, and at other locations throughout the book, are a number of frequently asked questions about political issues. After each question is a typical response from a liberal, a conservative and a libertarian. We will begin with some of the questions raised by *The World's Smallest Political Quiz.*

Because liberals do not all think alike and conservatives do not all think alike, the responses listed for them are naturally subject to challenge by any liberal or conservative who might disagree. However, the liberal and conservative responses are based on the experience of the author who has heard or read the statements and positions of thousands of people who described themselves as either liberals or conservatives. The libertarian responses are based upon the writings of libertarian scholars, the author's personal views, and the Libertarian Party Platform.

COMPARING LIBERAL, CONSERVATIVE AND LIBERTARIAN

* Should there be conscription, a draft, for military purposes?
Liberal: Yes, but not in peace time.
Conservative: Yes, America must always be strong to deter potential enemies and young people need it to learn patriotism.
Libertarian: Absolutely not, under any circumstances. The draft is slavery. Slaves make poor defenders of freedom.

* Should government own or control newspapers, radio or television?
Liberal: Yes. We need PBS to make sure there is some high quality programming and government should control advertising aimed at children and other gullible people.
Conservative: Government should not own the press or TV but should control it to prevent obscene programs and to ensure balanced reporting by the liberal dominated media.
Libertarian: No. Government ownership or control of press or electronic media has no place in a free society. Owners of papers and broadcasters should be responsible for what they publish. Let parents and other consumers be responsible for what to allow into their homes.

* Should government regulate any sexual activity of consenting adults, including prostitution?
Liberal: Generally not. But, if prostitution were legal, it should be regulated to protect public health.
Conservative: Yes. Prostitution, homosexuality, adultery and fornication should all be illegal because they destroy family values.
Libertarian: No. Sexual activity involving consenting adults violates the rights of no other person. The right of adults to make their own decisions in this most private area must be respected.

* Should drugs like marijuana, cocaine and heroin be legalized?
Liberal: A qualified yes. Start slowly, perhaps with marijuana first, but the production and sale should be regulated and taxed. Tax money should be used for drug treatment programs.
Conservative: NO! Are you nuts? Everyone knows that everything bad in the world is caused by drugs, dope dealers and stoned out gangs. What we need is stricter laws and more prisons.
Libertarian: Yes. Peaceful drug use violates no other person's rights. People have the right to control their own bodies. The drug laws support organized crime, cause more crime, corrupt law enforcement, destroy civil rights, and DO NOT WORK! (See Chapter 10.)

* Should it be legal for people to travel or move into and out of the U.S. without limitation?

Liberal: We should give more help to people trying to escape poverty and political oppression so they can to come to America, but not without limitation because they take jobs from Americans.

Conservative: No. We have too many immigrants already. Everyone will want to come to America. They increase welfare costs, take our jobs, increase crime and disease, and refuse to learn English.

Libertarian: Yes. All individuals have the same rights, regardless of where they were born or where they live now. Anyone willing to take responsibility for himself or herself has the right to travel and seek opportunity, including across international borders. America has always benefitted from immigrants who arrive with nothing, work hard, start businesses, become educated and improve America's economy.

For more information, see the *Bibliography of Suggested Reading* at the end of the book.

CHAPTER SIX
LIBERTARIAN ANALYSIS OF THE ISSUES

To examine any particular issue from the libertarian point of view, two factors must be considered: the "moral" and the "practical."

THE MORAL ELEMENT

The "moral" portion of the analysis requires that we examine the status of the people in the situation under examination to determine whether they are dealing with each other in a peaceful, voluntary and honest manner. If they are, no one is violating the rights of any other. In such cases it would be immoral for anyone to bring force into the situation. If one of the participants is using force (or the threat of it) against the other participants, that means those others are having their rights violated. The aggressive use of force should be stopped. It would be moral to use government force to assist those persons whose rights are being violated by such aggressive use of force against them.

To a libertarian, the answer to the moral question is primary. Determining the moral or the right course of action is of utmost importance. Traditional politicians almost never deal with the question of whether government force is being used properly (to assist citizens in defending their rights) or improperly (in a way which violates the citizens' rights). A libertarian will always raise that question and argue against the use of government force in any instance other than to assist the citizen in self defense.

THE PRACTICAL ELEMENT

The second consideration is the "practical" question. This involves considerations and predictions of what people will do in response to a particular law, regulation, or government policy. Most political discussions today deal only with the practical issue and completely ignore the moral issue.

The "practical" analysis only asks whether, if a specific law is passed, people will do what the legislators intend. Consider these examples: If the law imposes criminal penalties on employers who hire illegal aliens, will employers discriminate against all aliens, legal and illegal? If taxes are reduced, will that induce greater productivity on the part of business and workers? If the minimum wage law is lowered from $4.25 per to $3.00 per hour, will that induce employers to hire more unskilled teenagers? If ownership of handguns is made illegal, will that reduce crime? If criminal penalties for possession of marijuana are eliminated, will that reduce crime or induce millions more to become marijuana users? If trade barriers are reduced or eliminated, will that hurt or help the U.S. economy?

Typically, political discussions about proposals for new legislation or repeal of existing laws deal only with "practical" considerations. We have all become accustomed to politicians and political commentators limiting themselves in this way and so it sounds odd when someone, usually a libertarian, questions whether a proposal to use government force in a given instance is morally justified.

It is rare when the moral issue becomes part of the general public discussion. The issue of the morality of the draft for military purposes is one of those rare instances. During the Vietnam War, and today with the legal obligation to register for the draft, some people raise the question of whether is it moral to impose criminal penalties on young men who refuse to register or be drafted. Prior to the war between the states, the morality of an established legal institution and practice was challenged by the libertarians of that day. This was the abolitionists' challenge to the moral legitimacy of slavery. The current debate over abortion is also rare in that it is being fought primarily as a "moral" issue with both sides arguing in terms of "rights".

The following chapters contain a series of brief discussions on a number of important political issues for today. These discussions are presented from a libertarian point of view and the analyses will contain both moral and practical considerations.

One of the nagging questions in many peoples' minds, even if they find the morality of freedom appealing, is whether or not it is practical. People want to know if freedom will work. With fewer governmental restrictions of their actions, will people be able to deal effectively with the problems that arise in their lives?

Libertarians are working for freedom, not only because it is morally right, but also because freedom is infinitely more practical than the political conditions prevailing today. In other words, the more freedom we have, the greater is the opportunity for each of us to achieve goals and values of our own choosing.

COMPARING LIBERAL, CONSERVATIVE AND LIBERTARIAN

* Should the government provide price supports and other subsidies to farmers and regulate what they grow?
Liberal: Yes. Farmers need protection from low prices for their crops and these farm programs help supply food to the poor and needy.
Conservative: Some support is needed so that family farms are not lost but, in general, farm programs are too expensive and wasteful.
Libertarian: No. No one in business is entitled to have the government force taxpayers to support him. Farmers should operate in a free, competitive market, just as all others in business should.

* Should the government impose tariffs, quotas or other restrictions on international trade, or should we have free trade?
Liberal: Tariffs and quotas should be used to save American jobs.
Conservative: Trade barriers may be necessary to protect industries vital to national defense or keep American industry competitive.
Libertarian: Trade barriers violate the rights of Americans and foreign people who desire to trade. Trade barriers cut everyone's productivity and cost more jobs than they save. (See Chapter 7.)

* Should government set a minimum wage enforced by law?
Liberal: Yes. Otherwise, employers will exploit workers by paying only subsistence wages. Everyone is entitled to a decent wage.
Conservative: No. Employers should be able to hire the best employees they can get at the lowest price set by market competition.
Libertarian: No. Such laws violate the right of employees and employers to strike their own deals. Economics and history show that minimum wage laws cause unemployment. (See Chapter 12.)

* Is there something fundamentally wrong with taxation, which all seem to think is the only way to pay for government services?
Liberal: Without taxes, not enough people would be willing to pay for welfare for the poor, or education, or taking care of the environment, or so many other important things which only government can provide.
Conservative: Without taxes, not enough people would be willing to pay for America's and its allies defense, or for our domestic security, or so many other important things only government can provide.
Libertarian: Taxation is immoral, indistinguishable from theft. We should replace taxation with voluntary methods of providing services. All "government" services can be provided by private sector business, charities or other organizations and techniques. (See Chapter 8.)

CHAPTER SEVEN

FOREIGN POLICY, FREE TRADE AND NUCLEAR ARMS

Libertarian foreign policy can be summed up in this phrase: neutrality, free trade, nuclear arms reduction and responsible defense. Compare this to the bipartisan policy followed by the leadership of the Democratic and Republican parties for the past several decades. Their bipartisan policy has been foreign interventionism, nuclear arms buildup, and a variety of legal restrictions on the right of American and other people to trade peacefully and honestly with each other.

SECURITY, LIBERTY, PROSPERITY

A foreign policy should be based on and tested by some relevant criteria. In the author's view, there are three main considerations: (1) the effects on the security of Americans from the possibility of an attack by a foreign power; (2) the effects on the personal liberties of Americans from governmental measures taken in the name of national security; and (3) the effects on the prosperity of Americans due to taxes and government spending for military purposes.

NEUTRALITY: NON-INTERVENTION

The first element in the libertarian foreign policy is neutrality or, as some people might say, non-intervention. The U.S. government is not the government of the world and has no authority to act as a government (militarily, economically or otherwise) in other parts of the world. The globe is covered with governments of sovereign nations, each having authority over its own area.

In recent decades, Democratic and Republican party leaders have apparently thought that they could go anywhere in the world and do anything to anyone so long as they could get away with it. A reversal of the situation demonstrates how absurd and dangerous this idea is. If some citizens of Iraq, for instance, were to be travelling in America and were arrested and accused of breaking the law in Chicago, and if Iraqi soldiers were to invade Chicago with the intent to rescue those Iraqi citizens, all America would be an uproar, declaring that this was an act of war justifying the most serious reprisals from the U.S. government against Iraq. Those objections would be valid. The U.S. government's interventions in other countries are equally unjustified.

But, it might be argued, what if the U.S. is requested to come to the aid

31

of another country, such as the government of El Salvador, which asks for U.S. assistance against Marxist rebels in that country? Or perhaps a request from the government of Saudi Arabia that the U.S. military install itself there to protect against a potential invasion by Iraq? Such events would still not justify U.S. government intervention on behalf of the group requesting the aid. In any dispute in a foreign country there will be at least two factions, and more often several, as in the cases of Lebanon and Cambodia. The existing "government" is just one of those factions.

If given a choice, some American citizens would back one faction, some would back another, and some, probably the great majority, would prefer not to be involved at all. But, if the U.S. government intervenes to help one faction, it forces all Americans to support that faction because our taxes are financing the U.S. government's intervention. This violates the rights of all those Americans who would have made a different choice.

Further, in such interventions, the U.S. government increases the possibility that all Americans will be drawn into greater war, jeopardizing our security. Such intervention also generates hostility and resentment toward all Americans wherever they may be, thus increasing the risk that Americans outside U.S. borders will be killed, terrorized or taken hostage.

Libertarians advocate that the U.S. government adopt a policy of neutrality toward other governments and withdraw from all military alliances or commitments by the U.S. government to take military action on behalf of other governments.

The U.S. government's primary legitimate function is to provide security for Americans from the risk that some foreign power or powers will attack them. American defense should provide security for the American people at home.

MILITARY WELFARE FOR WEALTHY COUNTRIES

For decades, the U.S. government has stationed hundreds of thousands of military personnel overseas, 325,000 in Western Europe, 45,000 in South Korea, more in Japan, the Philippines and numerous other locations. As this is being written, as many as 200,000 American troops are moving into Saudi Arabia in response to Iraq's invasion of Kuwait. For some time the U.S. military budget has been about 300 billion dollars per year, about 65% of which is for military expenditures in other parts of the world, primarily Western Europe and the Pacific. The average working taxpayer in West Germany or Japan pays less for the defense of his country than the average working taxpayer in America pays for the defense of Germany or Japan. American taxpayers are being forced to support a military welfare program for other wealthy countries. (This obviously affects the ability of American companies to compete in international markets with Japanese and German companies which have a lighter tax burden due to the U.S. defense subsidy.)

American military personnel should be brought home to defend Americans and their property here. And that can be done with substantially reduced numbers. A look at a map of the world and the realities of the world situation demonstrate that there is no probability of a conventional military attack against the United States. No country or group of countries has any plan whatsoever to invade the U.S. If any such attempt were made, it would surely and quickly fail. The only military risk still facing the United States is the increasingly remote possibility of a Soviet nuclear attack, which we will address later.

U.S. surface naval forces should also be returned to American coastal areas from their deployments around the world. The recent U.S. naval buildup, based on the policy of interventionism, is designed to enable the U.S. to be involved in several wars concur-rently around the world. That policy should end, and with it the deployment of conventional U.S. naval forces on a global scale.

FREE TRADE: PEACE AND PROSPERITY

Free trade is the second essential element in the libertarian foreign policy. Libertarians advocate free trade for several reasons. The most basic is that individuals have the right to engage in economic or commercial transactions with each other on any basis which is peaceful, voluntary and honest. It does not matter whether the participants in this economic activity are located in the same city, the same state, different states, or different countries. As human beings, each has the right to offer goods and services to willing buyers. No one has the right to step in between them with a gun and penalize them or prevent them from engaging in peaceful and honest trade. The existence of an international boundary does not change this principle.

Free trade is a powerful inducement to international peace. Any time a trade barrier is removed, increased trade follows and the people who engage in it are more prosperous. When people in different countries are able to trade freely with each other, they do not want their beneficial trade relationships interrupted by war.

It is an interesting historical fact that the U.S. government has never gone to war with another government while free trade relationships existed between them. History also shows us that governments tend to follow the lead of other governments where trade barriers are concerned. If one government lowers its trade barriers, others tend to respond in kind. If one government raises its trade barriers, others tend to retaliate. Thus, if the U.S. government seeks to induce other governments to reduce their trade barriers, the most practical policy is immediate removal of all U.S. trade barriers (tariffs, quotas, etc.) which limit peaceful, honest trade between Americans and people in other countries. Removing trade restrictions would be the single most efficient way to improve the prosperity of Americans and others, and to improve the relationships between Americans and people of different countries.

It should also be noted that a capable defense for any country depends upon a productive economy to finance that defense. To the degree that other countries, such as those in Central America, become more prosperous as a result of increased trade with Americans, they will be better able to defend themselves. Further, as prosperity and friendly relationships with Americans improve due to increased trade, the appeal of socialism is reduced.

NUCLEAR ARMS POLICIES

During the "Cold War" period since World War II, the only significant military risk to the American people has been the possibility of a nuclear attack from the Soviet Union. The U.S. and the Soviets conducted a costly and dangerous nuclear arms race. Until quite recently, it appeared there would be no end to it. Unfortunately, the leaders of both the Democratic and Republican parties seemed unable to agree on an analysis of the situation, or even on policies which would slow the increase in nuclear arms. Now it appears that the worldwide collapse of socialist economies, including the Soviet economy, the collapse of the Warsaw Pact, and the continuing political disintegration of the Soviet Union itself, has ended the Cold War and the nuclear arms race. But, the nuclear arsenals still exist, as does the risk that they might be used.

Both the U.S. and the Soviets have huge strategic nuclear arsenals. Both sides maintain and manifest some reluctance to reduce their nuclear arsenals, operating on theories which aim at avoiding nuclear war, or if it cannot be avoided, surviving in a condition superior to the other side.

Analysts tell us that the Soviet strategic policy is the "preemptive first strike." This means that if the Soviet leaders perceive a great risk of attack, they will strike first, aiming at the U.S. missiles and other military and political installations in an attempt to destroy the ability of the U.S. to retaliate or defend against a subsequent invasion. Millions of Americans would die under such a scenario.

During the Cold War period, the Soviets followed an "expansionist" policy. This is understandable (though not justifiable) because of Russian history. Russia has been invaded several times (even by the U.S. during World War I) and wants to protect its country and people from such terrible devastation happening again. The Soviets have sought to maintain a buffer of client states (the Warsaw Pact) on their borders to discourage any potential invaders of the Soviet homeland. Soviet policy is to strike first if it appears that any country or group of countries is seriously preparing to attack the Soviet Union.

By contrast, the stated U.S. nuclear policy is "deterrence" based upon the ability to retaliate after a Soviet first strike; to retaliate so completely as to destroy everything of value in the Soviet Union. The death toll on the Soviet civilian population in the event of such a retaliatory strike would be many tens of millions, a circumstance which libertarians find morally unacceptable.

MASSIVE NUCLEAR ARSENALS

The U.S. strategic nuclear arsenal is made up of three types of missiles: land based, submarine carried, and bomber carried. Any one of these three components is maintained in sufficient numbers to destroy the Soviet Union several times. Therefore, it is possible to eliminate a great many U.S. missiles of each type and still retain the ability to retaliate pursuant to the policy of deterrence.

In addition to the "strategic" nuclear missiles, the U.S. has deployed in Europe a number of "tactical" nuclear missiles. The difference is that the tactical missiles in Europe have a shorter range and are not capable of intercontinental flight as are the Strategic missiles. These tactical missiles are deployed in Europe under the control of the U.S. government as part of the NATO alliance of Western European countries and the United States. The Soviets also have tactical nuclear missiles stationed in Eastern Europe as part of the Warsaw Pact military arsenal.

NUCLEAR WAR FIGHTING FOLLY

In the event that war begins in Europe between the communist Warsaw Pact countries and the Western European NATO countries, the United States is committed to use its tactical nuclear weapons. In addition to the U.S.-NATO tactical nuclear weapons, England and France also have medium range nuclear weapons. Because of its control over these weapons in Europe, the United States has deviated from its stated strategic nuclear policy of deterrence and has moved toward a policy of limited nuclear war fighting. In other words, U.S. military and political leaders believe that it will be possible to engage in nuclear war on a limited scale and "win" it!

The author believes that this is governmental folly more dangerous than any other in history. It is much more probable that if the first U.S. or Soviet tactical nuclear weapons are used, the rest of the U.S. and Soviet missiles would also be used.

Fortunately, in the past year or two, Europe has changed dramatically, reducing to near zero the prospects of a Warsaw Pact or Soviet invasion of Western Europe. Eastern Europeans have rejected communism as an ideology and no government there has the remotest interest in military confrontation. As a practical matter, the Warsaw Pact no longer exists. U.S. and Soviet negotiators are rapidly moving toward massive reductions of nuclear weapons on both sides and substantial reductions of conventional forces as well. We should all encourage American political leaders to support and accelerate these welcome developments.

"STAR WARS"

Another significant element in the current nuclear arena is the continuing research and development of defensive anti-ballistic missile systems. In 1983, President Reagan gave what has come to be known as his "Star Wars" speech, in which he advocated the development of space based antimissile systems. The term now used to describe such systems and government policy is "Strategic Defense Initiative" or SDI. The argument in favor of this development is that SDI technology would be a beneficial replacement for weapons of mass destruction, a truly "defensive" system to replace deterrence by the threat of retaliatory destruction. The arguments against such a system have been that, technologically, it is always easier and less expensive to develop the offensive capability to penetrate a defense shield; the expense would be astronomical; and the Soviets would probably perceive such developments as effectively disarming them so they would be more likely to make a preemptive strike while it could still be effective. Further, many leading U.S. scientists contend that the development of such a system is technologically impossible, at least for many decades.

Recent reductions in tensions between the U.S. and the Soviet Union obviously call for a reevaluation of anti-SDI arguments insofar as they are premised on the need to prepare for a massive first strike from the Soviets.

NUCLEAR ARMS REDUCTION AND SDI

In light of current circumstances, the author advocates the following policies regarding nuclear weapons:

1. The U.S. should make a clear declaration of "no first use" of nuclear weapons. This applies primarily to the tactical nuclear weapons in Europe and should be done in connection with a U.S. withdrawal from the NATO alliance.

2. Terminate U.S. control of tactical nuclear weapons in Europe. If the Western Europeans feel that tactical nuclear weapons are necessary for their defense, they should develop them and take full responsibility for them. The U.S. finger should be removed from the nuclear trigger in Europe.

3. Immediately begin the elimination of all land based missiles in the United States while continuing to rely for strategic deterrence on the submarine and bomber carried missiles. This would make Americans more secure for two reasons. First, it would remove land based missiles in America as potential targets for a Soviet first strike. Second, it would constitute an unmistakable commitment to the process of nuclear arms reduction, thus further reducing tensions.

4. Negotiations with the Soviets to participate in mutual nuclear arms reduction should continue and be acted upon. Every Soviet offer to

remove or destroy any number of nuclear weapons should be accepted. Since 1983, the Soviets have taken the lead with offers to either stop the new deployment of nuclear missiles or remove existing ones. Sadly, it has been the U.S. which has been slow to respond to these offers. It now appears that the Soviet offers were sincere.

In the past, negotiations with the Soviets have bogged down, in part, due to the unwillingness of either side to make any reductions without precisely equal reductions on the other side. Thus, negotiations were agonizingly slow due to arguments over whether elimination of a given warhead or launching device was technologically equal to something the other side was willing to eliminate. The U.S. does not have to lock itself in to demands for precise equality in arms reduction. The security of Americans will be improved by implementing the policies discussed here even if Soviet nuclear reductions were to lag behind. Indeed, a realistic appraisal of the current situation indicates that it is the Soviets who are setting the pace and that the U.S. is the laggard.

In the context of implementation of libertarian policies of neutrality, of conventional military withdrawal from around the world, of free trade, of nuclear arms reduction, and the de facto end of the Cold War, we can fairly comfortably conclude that there would be no further significant risk of a first strike from the Soviets.

In such a context, it would make sense to continue the research and development of defensive anti ballistic missile technology, *but only in such* a context. Until the U.S. government withdraws from its belligerent interventionism and its self-appointed role as world policeman, it would be imprudent to work on developing SDI, as that would be perceived by many countries as more evidence of U.S. intentions to dominate them militarily.

ADVANTAGES OF LIBERTARIAN POLICIES

Now let us compare the existing bi-partisan Democratic and Republican foreign policy of military intervention, nuclear arms proliferation, and protectionist trade barriers to the libertarian policy of neutrality, military withdrawal, nuclear arms reduction and free trade. Consider the relevant criteria: the effects on the security of Americans, the effects on the personal liberties of Americans, and the effects on the economic well-being of Americans.

Under libertarian policies, the security of Americans would greatly increase because of further reductions in tensions between the U.S., the Soviets and third world governments (particularly the Arab countries) and due to the development of peaceful and friendly relations between Americans and people in foreign countries resulting from increased trade.

Regarding our personal liberties at home, the most significant effect would probably be elimination of the threat of a military draft and draft registration, thus freeing millions of young men from that particularly vicious violation of their liberties. Further, as we reduce military involvement of the U.S. government abroad, we reduce government surveillance of American citizens in the name of national security. (During the Vietnam war, the C.I.A. and the F.B.I. infiltrated and disrupted political organizations opposed to U.S. involvement in that war.)

The improvement in the prosperity of Americans from adopting a libertarian foreign policy would be tremendous. First, reductions in military spending would mean much lower taxes. Recall that approximately two-thirds of the current military budget is spent abroad. The distortion of the economy due to so much American productive effort being directed toward military matters would be reduced. Obviously, the prosperity of Americans would greatly increase due to improvement in trade relationships with other people throughout the world.

THE DISASTER OF INTERVENTION

By comparison, the bipartisan interventionist policies of the Democrats and Republicans have been a disaster for American security. The greatest disaster is the waste of young Americans lives.

The pattern of U.S. foreign military intervention is typically as follows: In some part of the world different factions are involved in a dispute. The U.S. government decides to assist one faction and sends U.S. military personnel to the area. A number of young Americans are killed. A number of other people are killed. Eventually, the U.S. military is pulled out and then things go back to the way they were before.

In addition to the death and maiming of many young Americans, U.S. interventionism typically generates resentment and hatred toward the U.S. government and innocent American citizens, putting them at risk while abroad, in particular. Finally, the American taxpayer bears the tax burden for the operation, and sometimes for a long time afterwards, to support the remaining "approved" faction in the area.

IRAQ AND PERSIAN GULF OIL

Until recently, many people were concerned that if the U.S. were to withdraw from military commitments around the world this would create a vacuum which the Soviets would immediately fill. With the elimination of the Soviet threat, interventionists are looking for other bogeymen to justify worldwide U.S. military involvement. Right on cue, Iraq's army invades Kuwait and threatens Saudi Arabia, seizing Americans and other westerners to use as hostages and human shields to protect Iraqi military and political targets. Iraq's Saddam Hussein is likened to Hitler and the world community, following the U.S. lead, takes action to stop Iraq. But note, it is American soldiers, male and female, who are put at risk in the

Saudi desert. Military contingents from other countries, even moderate Arab countries in the vicinity, are insignificant by comparison to the American presence. It is predictable that the same old pattern will play itself out in the Persian Gulf.

It would be nice if aggressors such as Iraq could be stopped cold at no cost. (Ironically, when Iraq was the aggressor against Iran, the U.S. government was aiding Iraq.) But there is always a cost, and it is too high. The argument that Persian Gulf oil supplies are in jeopardy and the U.S. must protect them will not fly. Even if (a very big if) Iraq were to capture and control Kuwait's and Saudi Arabia's oil fields, they are of no value to Iraq unless the oil is sold on the world market. In the absence of the U.S. military intervention, the disruption of oil reaching the international market would have been of short duration and not very substantial as other suppliers around the world increased production rapidly to profit from reduced oil supplies from the Persian Gulf. It is the U.S. military intervention itself, and the resulting threat of widespread and long term war in the area which threatens the international oil supply system and drives up prices. If the international free market in oil were allowed to work, the oil supply disruption would probably be much less serious than it is with the U.S. military intervention.

When the supply of any commodity is interrupted in a free market, prices increase and give a signal to people to alter their conduct. Other suppliers increase production and consumers conserve and look for alternatives. It is when the government interferes and doesn't allow the market to work in response to the disruption that problems are made worse and take longer to solve. A good example is the "gas lines" we all waited in during the 1970s when the government tried to allocate and ration gasoline rather than letting competition in the marketplace do it. In short, leaving things alone would cost us less in lives, tax dollars, and oil prices than military intervention.

AN END TO MILITARY WELFARE

As pointed out above, the defense of the wealthy countries of Europe, Japan, South Korea, and others, now including Saudi Arabia, is currently being financed by the long-suffering American taxpayer. These countries are fully capable of deciding for themselves what military risks they face, what they want to do about it, and what they are willing to pay to protect themselves. They have the economic and military capability. They should take the responsibility. Clearly it is not the obligation of the American taxpayer to continue to support the rest of the western world on military welfare.

For more information, see the **Bibliography of Suggested Reading** at the end of the book.

COMPARING LIBERAL,
CONSERVATIVE AND LIBERTARIAN

* Inflation is a recurring problem, when we see prices rising rapidly. What should the Federal Government do about it?
Liberal: Impose wage and price controls and controls on interest rates to keep big corporations and banks from gouging the public.
Conservative: The Federal Reserve Board should increase the money supply at a slow and steady rate and control interest rates also rather than allowing wide fluctuations in either.
Libertarian: We must stop the government money printing press. Return now to a fully convertible gold standard for the dollar and ultimately establish a stable, market-based monetary system to replace government control of money by eliminating the Federal Reserve system and repealing the legal tender laws.

* Should the U.S. Government send troops or other military agents to intervene in the affairs of other countries?
Liberal: Yes, if it will advance the cause of human rights.
Conservative: Yes, if it will help contain the spread or resurgence of communism or protect other U.S. interests such as oil.
Libertarian: No. The U.S. government has no authority to intervene militarily in the affairs of other countries except in response to a military attack on the American homeland. (See Chapter 7.)

* Should the United States Government send foreign aid to other countries?
Liberal: Yes, to help the poor in third world and developing countries which have good human rights records.
Conservative: Yes, to help those governments trying to resist communism or trying to convert from socialism to democracy.
Libertarian: No. American taxpayers should not be forced to pay to support other governments at all. (See Chapter 7.)

* Should the United States Government continue to participate in and support the United Nations?
Liberal: Yes, because it is the last best hope for peace.
Conservative: Yes, but only if it will take a more pro-American stance.
Libertarian: Not as presently constituted and financed by tax dollars. A voluntarily financed forum for international discussions would not be objectionable. (See Chapter 7.)

CHAPTER EIGHT
TAXATION AS THEFT

> To lay with one hand the power of the
> government on the property of the citizen
> and with the other to bestow it upon favored
> individuals to aid private enterprises and
> build up private fortunes is none the less a
> robbery because it is done under the forms
> of law and is called taxation.
>
> United States Supreme Court,
> *Savings and Loan Association v.Topeka*

Libertarians do not make a distinction between people in government
and people outside government. All people are subject to the same moral
standards. The topic of which government functions are legitimate, such
as national defense and protecting constitutional rights, is a separate topic
from the question of moral or immoral methods of financing these functions.

The traditional financing method for government is called "taxation",
and taxation is as old as the institution of the state. In his book, *The State*,
Franz Oppenheimer showed that the development of the state as an
institution was based on tribal conquests and the exaction of tribute by the
conquerors from the conquered people. Invariably one tribe or group
would conquer another and require the conquered peoples to pay in crops,
labor, or other property on a continuing basis. In return, the conquerors
would typically protect the conquered people from other marauding
tribes. The protection money paid by the conquered peoples came to be
called taxation.

Libertarians are willing to call taxation by its accurate name: "theft".
Taxation is simply some people using the force at their disposal to steal the
earnings or property of other people. The taxpayer-victim is threatened
with fines or jail if he refuses to pay. If the taxpayer resists the government's thievery, the tax enforcing officials have the power (not the moral
right) to crush the resistance with whatever force is necessary, including
lethal force.

DOES IMMORAL THEFT BECOME MORAL TAXATION
BECAUSE THE GANG GETS LARGER?

If a man with a gun came to your house or place of business and told
you to deliver to him a portion of your weekly earnings upon penalty of

being locked up or shot if you resisted, you would consider that a clear violation of your rights and properly label it "armed robbery". You would be justifiably incensed at the injustice of such an action. If the same man came with 10, or 100, or 1,000 accomplices, it is unlikely your opinion would change.

If the robber told you he intended to do good things with the money, such as, defending you from other robbers, or providing education for poor children, or feeding hungry refugees overseas, you would be justified in rejecting these transparent rationalizations. Regardless of what a thief plans to do with the loot, theft is immoral and cannot be condoned in a sane society.

The underlying facts and principles do not change when the process of theft is obscured by politics and legalisms. Just because a group of legislators assert, by "passing a law", that you must submit to their thievery, and just because they have men with guns at their disposal to compel you to submit, the immoral nature of the process called taxation does not change.

One important libertarian goal is to show that taxation is based on coercion, and to encourage people of good will everywhere to join in efforts to eliminate coercive taxation as the method for financing legitimate government functions. There are alternatives for financing government which do not involve coercion, but rather are based upon respect for the rights of the people and voluntary cooperation.

ELIMINATE CRIMINAL PENALTIES

One particularly damning indictment of government is that it enforces the tax code with criminal penalties. People who do not file tax returns or pay taxes according to the code may be jailed. A taxpayer, even one without assets, cannot file bankruptcy and discharge a tax liability in the same way private debts are discharged.

As private citizens, we cannot threaten those who owe us money with jail. We can only bring civil lawsuits and collect after a trial and judgment. And if our debtors are insolvent, they can file bankruptcy and eliminate their debts. An immediate, interim reform to our tax laws should be to remove the criminal penalties and put government tax collectors in the same status as any private citizen trying to collect a debt.

THE FEDERAL INCOME TAX

Let's look at the Federal Income Tax, the most familiar tax to all of us. The Sixteenth Amendment to the U.S. Constitution was adopted in 1913, making it possible (according to questionable Supreme Court decisions) for the U.S. government to tax the income of the citizens directly. The income tax went into effect in 1914.

During the debates in Congress over whether to have a federal income tax, some argued that since there was no upper limit on the tax Congress could impose, the income tax might go as high as 10% of a person's income. They were hooted down as alarmists, but they were right. Income tax rates have gone as high as 91%! The U.S. Supreme Court has held that there is no constitutional impediment to Congress imposing an income tax of 100%, and that for Congress to leave the citizens with any portion of their earnings is merely a matter of "legislative grace".

SURVIVE WITHOUT THE INCOME TAX?

Is it possible for Americans to survive without the income tax? There is every reason to believe we could. Remember, the federal income tax has been part of our law only since 1914. Before that time the people of America prospered. By the year 1900, Americans were first in the world in per capita wealth and standard of living, a time when immigration rates where much higher than today.

Since 1914, and especially since World War II, the federal government has grown fantastically and the federal income tax has risen to astronomical proportions. The federal income tax accounts for between one-third and forty percent of the total amount of money that the federal government spends each year. If the federal government were confined to its legitimate functions of national defense and the protection of constitutional rights, the federal income tax could be eliminated. And, of course, if that were accomplished, it would also be able to abolish the one federal agency most feared by Americans, the Internal Revenue Service.

SOME ALTERNATIVES TO THE INCOME TAX

The logical question to ask at this point is: How could government be financed if taxation were not available? In other words, if people weren't forced to support government, would they do it, and how?

As this book is written, the federal budget plans appear to be leading us toward an unbelievable total of about $1.3 trillion. Ten years ago, the federal budget was less than half that sum. Of that total, military spending will account for about $300 billion. Also, there is a budget deficit anticipated in excess of $200 billion. That deficit will be financed by the U.S. government borrowing money in private financial markets. If the federal government were confined (as libertarians advocate) to providing national defense and protection of constitutional rights, federal expenditures could be reduced substantially, at least by two thirds and probably more. So the amount of voluntary financing necessary would only be a fraction of the current budgets paid for with taxation and deficits.

There are many possible methods for voluntary financing of the legitimate functions of the federal government. Private organizations in America raise well over $100 billion per year in money, material and services from people who are willing to support their efforts. We can learn from the voluntary fundraising methods these organizations use.

Most people agree that national defense and protection of constitutional rights are very important and would voluntarily support them. But most are also understandably reluctant to support many of the other things the U.S. government does. This is the main reason so many people object to paying taxes.

NATIONAL DEFENSE ENDOWMENT

One proposal for voluntary financing is to create a "national defense endowment fund". The U.S. government owns one-third of the land in America. It also owns a great many other valuable assets (Tennessee Valley Authority, other power plants, Amtrak, the Post Office resources, gold, silver, oil, etc.) none of which are necessary for the government's legitimate purposes. Portions of these assets could be sold off in order to raise the necessary sums to initiate a national defense endowment fund. Of course, all citizens would be encouraged to contribute voluntarily to the national defense endowment once it was established.

INSURANCE

Another possibility would be support from private insurance companies. Assume that insurance companies would write insurance to cover the risk of death, injury, or property damage resulting from an attack on the United States. Persons who bought such insurance would pay premiums to the insurance companies. When insurance companies write insurance to cover a specific risk they also often take other steps to reduce the possibility of having to pay off on that risk. For instance, fire insurance underwriters do research on fire safety, write building standards and codes, and inspect private and commercial occupancies all as part of a continuing program to reduce the amount they will have to pay due to fire loss. In the national defense area, it is probable that insurance companies would engage in a number of activities designed to improve the prospects for peace and effective defense against attack, such as contributing to research and development of defensive technology, subsidizing military training, intelligence gathering regarding potential enemies, and negotiations with foreign governments to improve international relations.

NATIONAL DEFENSE LOTTERY

Many state governments operate lotteries to raise money voluntarily, as an alternative to taxes. Thus, a "National Defense Lottery" is one more possibility for voluntary financing.

The foregoing suggestions are not intended as a complete list of possibilities. They merely illustrate that it is possible to develop voluntary methods of financing legitimate government functions as an alternative to taxation. The important point is that we, as compassionate and rational human beings, should acknowledge that the coercive method of government financing by taxation is immoral. And, therefore, our goal should be to replace the coercive method with voluntary methods more consistent with proper moral behavior. We may or may not be completely successful in reaching that goal, but it is the right goal.

COMPARING LIBERAL,
CONSERVATIVE AND LIBERTARIAN

* Should young Americans be compelled to serve in some capacity in the name of "national service"?

Liberal: Yes, everyone has the obligation to serve others for social welfare.

Conservative: Yes, when it can be justified for national defense purposes.

Libertarian: No. Slavery is slavery regardless of whether it is masked by the euphemism "draft" or "national service."

* Should the U.S. government bail out savings and loan institutions and banks to prevent their collapse?

Liberal: Yes, because all the depositors have depended on government deposit insurance to protect their savings.

Conservative: Yes, because if these financial institutions collapse, our entire economy will follow and it will be like the 1930s depression.

Libertarian: No. Taxpayers should not be compelled to bail out either financial institutions or individuals who make bad investments.

* Should the U.S. government help American businesses through hard economic times with low interest loans?

Liberal: Yes. This will save jobs and American workers need all the help they can get during a recession or depression.

Conservative: Yes. Government should help business stay in business. That's free enterprise.

Libertarian: No. Government can only help some businesses by stealing from taxpayers and other businesses. No one has the right to be subsidized at the expense of others. (See Chapter 8.)

* What is the best way to deal with the budget deficit problem?

Liberal: Raise taxes and reduce military spending.

Conservative: Don't raise taxes, but reduce social spending.

Libertarian: Reduce all federal spending. Confine the federal government to national defense and the protection of constitutional rights from violations by state and local governments.

*What is the best approach for dealing with problems of pollution?

Liberal: Stricter laws and better bureaucratic management paid for by tax dollars.

Conservative: Tax financed cleanup of industrial waste.

Libertarian: Respect for private property rights and legal protection against pollutants and polluters through traditional common law remedies of injunction and damages for trespass. (See Chapter 14)

For more information, see the *Bibliography of Suggested Readings* at the end of this book.

CHAPTER NINE

EDUCATION: STATE CONTROL OR FREEDOM OF CHOICE?

Everyone agrees it is important to provide young people with opportunities to develop their minds and learn about the world. It is also obvious that all children, from the youngest age, are eager to learn and continually seek intellectual stimulation. There is no way to stop children from developing their minds and taking in information about the world around them. The question is: "What will they learn, from whom, and in what circumstances?"

Most adult Americans have attended public, that is, government operated, schools and most American children now attend public schools. Unfortunately, there is a great deal of fault to find with the government operated schools, both on moral grounds and on the basis of poor results. It is no mere coincidence that the operation of the public schools is morally bankrupt and the results deplorable.

COERCION IS THE BASIS OF STATE RUN EDUCATION

Libertarians seek to remove coercion as the basis for human relationships. The relationship involving education is between suppliers and consumers of a service, just as in market situations. On the one side in public schools are the suppliers: administrators, teachers, custodians, building contractors, textbook publishers, etc. On the other side are the consumers: parents, children and taxpayers.

Human relationships in government schools are loaded with coercion. First, we have compulsory attendance laws. These laws make it a crime for parents to fail to deliver their children to school from age six to 17. Second, we have compulsory financing through taxation. The existence of these two laws, compulsory attendance and compulsory financing, establish a protected monopoly service business. Therefore, it should not be surprising that, as with all protected monopoly businesses, the public schools are terribly inefficient and expensive and not much concerned for the desires or welfare of the consumers.

Third, we have coercion regarding the subjects to be taught in the public schools. This explains the never ending battles over such things as prayer in school, sex education, creationism versus evolution, which books will be allowed in school libraries, and the contents of textbooks. Current textbooks tend to be a hodgepodge of bland materials which are the result of textbook editors and school authorities trying to satisfy, or not offend, a variety of interest groups.

Fourth, we have coercion regarding who can teach. Only certain persons with certain characteristics are allowed to teach under the current laws. For instance, a public school teacher who is homosexual, if discovered, is likely to be quickly out of a job. In many states, parents who prefer to teach their children at home are harassed by state school authorities. The same is true in many cases for people who want to provide religious schooling for their children.

Not long ago in Nebraska, seven fathers were jailed for contempt of court for educating their own children in a church school. The children were tested and scored higher than public school grade level and were willing to be tested regularly. The parents' only crime was that they refused to submit to the state's legal requirement that the operators of the school obtain the state's permission. State school authorities seem less interested in educational opportunity and quality than in establishing their power to control the mental development of the young to the exclusion of the parents.

GOALS OF STATE SCHOOLS

This should be no surprise. Before state schooling began in this country, literacy rates were quite high. In the early and mid-nineteenth century, professional educators promoted the idea of state schooling, primarily to insulate themselves from parental control. They were not much concerned for literacy or mental development of the young, that was already happening with private education. A second motive was to homogenize the population by using the state schools to remold immigrants, many of whom were Catholic, into obedient citizens who accepted the values of the dominant Protestant ethnic group.

The nineteenth century advocates of state schooling were quite clear in arguing that the children were not self-owners, but rather the property of the state. They contended that the function of the schools was to indoctrinate the children so that they would be patriotic, unquestioning, obedient citizens whose first loyalty was to the government; and that the primary obstacle to the achievement of these purposes was the interference of the students' parents and family. The state school system has been quite successful in achieving the end of molding generations of unquestioning, obedient servants to the state. It is equally clear that intellectual literacy, on all subjects, has declined in those same schools.

SEPARATION OF EDUCATION AND STATE

There is no proper role for government in education. One of the most valuable contributions to a peaceful and free society was made by the founders of this country when, in the First Amendment to the U.S. Constitution, they established the principle of separation of church and state. They were aware of centuries of religious war and persecution that resulted from attempts to establish state religions and to suppress dissenting views.

The right to freedom in the area of intellectual development and personal philosophy is fully as important as freedom of religion, and for the same reasons! Thus, there should be a separation of education and state just as there is a separation of church and state.

What are the results of government operated schools? In the last three decades, on average across the nation, the cost of operating government schools has increased nearly 1,000 percent, while enrollments declined, class sizes became smaller, student performance declined and violence and drug use increased. Today, nearly one out of four young people who graduate from or drop out of high school is a functional illiterate. Increasing numbers of adults are admitting they cannot read or write. Colleges and universities find that incoming freshmen need remedial training in reading, writing and critical analysis. Obviously, throwing more tax dollars at this failed system hasn't worked.

Children of poor and minority parents suffer most. Illiteracy in ghetto schools is as high as 40%. Across the nation, the average cost per student per year in public schools is about $5,000. In private schools, the average cost per student is about half that and private schools do a better job of educating. In public schools, violence and drug abuse is considerably higher than at private schools where these problems are virtually nonexistent

TAX CREDITS WILL BRING COMPETITION TO EDUCATION

As an interim measure (so long as the federal income tax exists), libertarians advocate tax credits for anyone who pays for the education of any student. Educational tax credits will improve education by introducing competition into the educational marketplace. A tax credit against federal income tax means a dollar reduction in tax liability for every dollar paid for education. The author specifically proposes a $2,500 per year, per student, tax credit for any person or any company who pays for the education of any student, or any number of students, at any school, public or private. The tax credit would not be limited to parents. Any wealthy individual or corporation could provide "scholarships" to as many students as they want, and reduce their taxes by the amount of the scholarships. The tax credit should be available for parents who teach their children at home as well.

Not only the parents of students, but also any wealthy individual or company could provide educational scholarships to students to broaden their educational choices at virtually no out-of-pocket cost due to the tax credit. This would bring competition into the educational marketplace, ending the protected monopoly position of government schools. It would also save the taxpayers money because each student who is educated on a

$2,500 tax credit in a private school saves the $5,000 cost in public school funding.

At first, we would expect to see a substantial move away from government schools and toward private educational alternatives. The government schools would have to respond by becoming more efficient, cutting their costs, and by being more responsive to the desires of the consumers of educational services, the parents and the students. This is as it should be. In an open, competitive market-place, only those who do the best job of satisfying consumer demand will survive. Open educational competition would also mean a great variety in subjects, systems and methods to meet the desires and requests of widely varied parents and students. The best teachers would be in great demand and their earnings would increase.

Libertarians have been advocating educational tax credits, or the similar education "voucher" system, for many years. Now mainstream politicians are picking up on this idea, calling for "choice" in education. Many school districts are experimenting by allowing students to attend any public school rather than being limited to the school closest to their home. The Wisconsin legislature has adopted a voucher system which allows the student to decide which school to attend, and that school gets the tax money for that student. In Oregon, an initiative proposition is on the ballot for the November 1990 general election which would establish an educational tax credit against the state income tax which is substantially identical to the author's proposal stated above.

BENEFITS FOR THOSE WHO NEED IT MOST

The children of the poor and minorities would benefit most from this educational tax credit which creates a source of direct private funding for them and thereby makes it possible for them to choose among many schools for the best educational bargain. Under the present system only the wealthy can afford to send their children to private schools while they also bear the tax burden for state schools. The inner city schools, attended primarily by poor and minority children, are the worst of a bad public school lot.

It may seem odd, but when libertarians make such proposals to improve educational opportunity by increasing freedom of choice, some people object that, if free to do so, some people might not send their children to school and those children would grow up ignorant. Or, that some poor people could not afford education for their children.

Such objections ignore the fact that the current system is producing a high percentage of failure, frustration, ignorance and illiteracy and that poor and minority children are the main victims. Compulsory attendance laws only require attendance, and many youngsters are so frustrated by what goes on in public schools that they not only do not learn themselves, they disrupt the learning process for other children.

Further, many poor parents are right now making tremendous sacrifices to escape the public schools and provide better educational opportunities for their children in private schools. And further, the libertarian educational tax credit proposal is not limited to parents; it is designed to encourage wealthy individuals and businesses to support education for poor students. An additional benefit of this will be to break down barriers between rich and poor; poor parents seeking education for their children and wealthy individual and corporate taxpayers seeking tax benefits will naturally come together for mutual benefit.

Finally, let us never forget that most important lesson: Utopia is not one of the options.

Our options are education based on coercion, or freedom of choice in education. For anyone with any honest concern and compassion for the young and their mental development, freedom of choice in education is the only answer.

COMPARING LIBERAL, CONSERVATIVE AND LIBERTARIAN

* The Social Security system keeps going bankrupt. Is there a long term solution to the problems of the Social Security system? Liberal: We will need to keep increasing the taxes because older people are entitled to retire with dignity.

Conservative: We need to reduce benefits, make the system more efficient, and make the age of retirement later to salvage it.

Libertarian: The Social Security bankruptcy requires we end the system by granting older workers and retirees the choice of a lump sum payment or private insurance annuity to replace future Social Security benefits. Ending the bankrupt system will relieve younger workers of the tax and avoid the economic collapse which will surely result from increasing Social Security taxes. (See Chapter 11.)

* Should children be required by law to attend schools?
Liberal: Yes, otherwise parents would not provide for their children's education.

Conservative: Yes, otherwise children will not be educated as required for national defense and to compete effectively in business with foreign companies.

Libertarian: No. Compulsory attendance laws violate the rights of parents and children to decide for themselves on educational programs. (See Chapter 9.)

* Should parents be allowed to teach their children at home rather than having them attend schools approved by the state?
Liberal: No. Some parents would teach their children bigotry and unscientific, bizarre religious doctrine.

Conservative: A grudging yes. Although some parents would fail to give their children the proper moral education with home schooling, it appears the public schools are hopeless for parents who want their children to have proper religious and moral education.

Libertarian: Yes. The government has no proper role in education. There should be no government penalties or regulation of parents who prefer to teach their children at home. (See Chapter 9.)

CHAPTER TEN

PROHIBITION REVISITED

The use of alcoholic beverages is as old as recorded history. At some times and places some people have sought to prevent others from producing, buying, selling or consuming alcoholic beverages. One such experiment was the period referred to as "Prohibition" in America from 1920 to 1933. The prohibition experiment is instructive because it shows so clearly the disastrous results of attempting to suppress peaceful activity with criminal law.

Possession of an alcoholic beverage does not violate the rights of any other person. To grow the grapes or grain from which liquor is made does not violate anyone's rights. To produce alcoholic beverages in a peaceful and honest manner violates no one's rights. Nor does drinking, buying or selling the liquor, violate the rights of any other person.

Libertarians say there is no justification for imposing criminal penalties on anyone who produces, buys, sells, possesses, or uses any intoxicating liquor. This conclusion naturally follows from basic libertarian analysis which recognizes that people own themselves and have the right to control their own lives, bodies, and honestly acquired property. People have the right to deal with each other in a peaceful and honest manner, including the production, use, and trade of alcoholic liquor. (This does not imply that libertarians say people should do any of these things. It means only that individual rights must be respected, and that to impose criminal penalties on people for exercising their rights in this way is not justified.)

NEGATIVE CONSEQUENCES OF CRIMINAL PENALTIES

What happens when criminal laws penalize people for peaceful activities? The experiences during Prohibition are a classic example and a lesson for today.

1. The law does not work. If people want to engage in a peaceful and honest activity, they will do it regardless of the law. Prohibition did not effectively prevent anyone from drinking alcoholic beverages. Today's drug laws do not prevent people from purchasing whatever drugs they want. Gun control laws do not prevent anyone who wants one from having a gun. Immigration laws are not stopping illegal immigrants from coming to the United States. Laws against homosexuality do not prevent homosexuals from having the relationships they desire.

2. Lives are ruined by making criminals out of peaceful people. Prohibition made Americans a nation of criminals. The current laws against drugs, prostitution, gambling, pornography, etc. have made criminals out of millions of peaceful Americans who are no threat to anyone.

One effect is that people already labeled as criminals may be willing to engage in other criminal activity.

3. The price of the illegal commodity is much higher than it would be in a competitive market. The law of supply and demand works in illegal as well as legal markets. By making a substance illegal, supply is reduced and the shortage causes higher prices. Consider the example from today's illegal drug market. Morphine and heroin are both opium derivatives, basically the same substance. An amount of morphine which costs $1.50 in the legal pharmaceutical market is equal to an amount of heroin that costs $100.00 in the illegal drug market. The difference in price is due solely to the difference in the law relating to the two opium derivatives.

4. Huge profits encourage criminal profiteers. Because of the high profits to be made in illegal markets, people willing to engage in crime are attracted to these illegal markets. Prohibition spawned organized crime. Organized crime continues to exist supported by illegal markets in drugs, prostitution, gambling, and pornography.

5. The existence of illegal markets corrupts the criminal justice system. To protect their huge profits, the criminal suppliers buy off police, courts and jailers in order to escape the effects of the law. Some police become drug dealers themselves or use their position to steal money and contraband from the illegal dealers or the evidence lockers. A sick, symbiotic relationship develops between lawmen and drug dealers. Evidence in a current criminal prosecution against several Los Angeles County Sheriff Deputies shows a pattern of beatings, filing false police reports, lying in search warrant affidavits, planting evidence on suspects and stealing money. Ironically, drug users inside prisons seem to have no problem getting illegal drugs so long as they have the money to pay for them.

6. Law enforcement is more expensive for the taxpayer and misdirected as well. About one-half of the tax dollars spent for law enforcement and the criminal justice system is spent on the suppression of peaceful activities, i.e., on "victimless crimes". The courts and prisons are so clogged with drug dealing or possession cases that judges allow many perpetrators of real crimes such as assault, robbery and burglary to go free. Police busy harassing drug users are not available to work on preventing real crimes, the kind with victims.

7. The products and services in illegal markets are of a lower quality than in legal markets. During Prohibition, people sometimes became quite ill or even died from impurities or defects in the liquors they purchased. "Bathtub gin" was the name for this inferior quality liquor. Today consumers of illegal drugs, illegal sexual services, or participants in illegal gambling are jeopardized in a similar manner. In illegal markets, the quality of products is unknown to the consumer. In legal markets, businesses provide information about products and services, such as *Consumer Reports* and other magazines which rate consumer products. In illegal markets, consumers have no legal protection against fraud or shoddy products. You cannot complain to the authorities about being ripped off if what you bought was illegal in the first place.

8. **Competition in illegal markets is based on violence as opposed to offering the consumer better quality products in honest trade.** Prohibition was known for its violent gang wars over territories. It is the same today, especially in the illegal drug markets. Frequently, innocent victims are caught in the crossfire. Another example is the prostitution market where women are victimized by violence and must seek the protection of violent men to stay in business. Those victimized by violence while engaged in any illegal market activity cannot seek protection from law enforcement.

9. **Civil liberties suffer as frustrated enforcers tighten the screws.** Enforcers turn to entrapment, tax laws and violation of the citizens' constitutional protection against unlawful and unreasonable search and seizure. The current "war on drugs" hysteria demonstrates this. Peaceful citizens are harassed on the highways, the high seas and at the border. Everyone's financial privacy is being destroyed in the search for drug profits. We all face the prospect of having to submit to periodic urine tests and roadblocks. The police can seize property without due process of law merely on the claim that it was purchased with "drug money". The police can stop and search you if you appear to match a "profile" of drug couriers. Recent court decisions, particularly those of the Supreme Court, have in effect created a "drug exception" to your constitutional rights. The armed services are now being used against American citizens, putting Americans at war against themselves.

10. **Relations with foreign countries suffer.** If the demand for contraband exists in the U.S., foreigners will find ways to supply it. The U.S. government then puts pressure on foreign governments to crack down on their citizens. Ultimately, the U.S. military begins operations in those countries to smash illegal drug suppliers, some of whom invariably turn out to be government officials, as was the case with Manuel Noriega in Panama. The people in those countries are given one more reason to despise the U.S. and its people.

DRUG USE AND DRUG LAW HISTORY

Let us now turn our attention to today's drug laws. For purposes of this discussion let us define 'drug' as any substance which, when ingested, has a short term or long term effect on a person's body or mind. There are thousands of such substances. Some are legal and available to anyone without government permission such as caffeine, aspirin, nose drops, etc. Other substances are legal but available only through regulated pharmacies, usually as medicines prescribed by licensed physicians to deal with ailments both mental and physical. Many of these substances escape legal

55

channels and become part of the illegal drug market. Then there are substances which are completely illegal, such as marijuana, heroin, cocaine, LSD, PCP, and a variety of other manufactured substances. Those who advocate strong drug laws typically argue that such laws are needed to suppress crime associated with drug use. But such arguments have cause and effect exactly reversed. The crime associated with drugs is a result of the criminal law that makes them illegal and generates all of the results discussed above. Before 1914, there was virtually no limitation or regulation of drug use. Opium and its derivatives were freely available in a variety of forms. There were no significant criminal problems or social problems associated with these substances. Many people used a variety of drugs, including alcohol, regularly and lived normal productive lives.

One group of such people, Chinese immigrants in the western part of the country, played a role in the passage of drug laws. Many Chinese immigrated in the latter 19th and early 20th century to the western part of the U.S. where they worked building railroads and on other jobs. They used opium as their recreational drug.

The hard working Chinese were viewed as a threat by the organized labor movement in America, led at that time by Samuel Gompers. In an effort to discredit the Chinese and limit their immigration, Gompers and other labor leaders attacked the use of opium by the Chinese, referring to the hard working immigrants as the "yellow peril". These racist attacks were a major contributing factor to the passage of the Harrison Narcotics Act of 1914 which outlawed opium and its derivatives.

In the late 1930s, Congress passed a law against marijuana use and possession. During Prohibition, a large force of federal law enforcement officials had developed to deal with the illegal alcoholic beverage industry. With the end of Prohibition, these law enforcement bureaucrats were looking for jobs. Some of them chose marijuana (which had never been viewed as a social problem before) as a potential target. Their propaganda described marijuana as a great scourge of mankind and they finally succeeded in having it criminalized. The people seeking to outlaw marijuana were quite willing to engage in the most outrageous false propaganda to achieve their ends, as anyone who has seen the film *Reefer Madness* can attest.

Today marijuana is acknowledged as the number one cash crop in several states in the country. Thousands of ordinary people supplement their earnings by growing and selling marijuana. Estimates are that between 25 million and 40 million Americans use marijuana from time to time. Of course, the street price of marijuana would drop dramatically if the market were legal, and the variety and quality of marijuana would surely increase in response to legal consumer demand. The marijuana plant, also known as hemp, has been recognized in the past as of great value for other reasons. It was a primary material used to produce rope, it can be used to make a variety of fabrics, and is a better raw material for the production of paper than wood. Before marijuana was criminalized, the U.S. government encouraged farmers to grow it.

DRUG LAWS ENCOURAGE DRUG USE AND EXPERIMENTATION

Why is it that people who sell alcoholic beverages do not hang around high schools or junior high schools trying to interest the youngsters in liquor? Why is it that we hear so much about illegal drugs like marijuana, cocaine, and heroin on high school campuses?

What we find is this pattern. A person who is a regular drug user has an expensive habit. One easy way for him to finance his habit is to develop a group of customers who buy from him. Such a person thus is motivated to give free samples to his young friends in order to make regular customers of them. Further, because under our criminal justice system juveniles are not subject to the same heavy penalties as adults, drug dealers protect themselves by having juveniles in their distribution system. Therefore, we can see that because of the high price of illegal drugs, caused by the fact that the use and possession of these drugs is a crime, there are natural incentives to increase use of these drugs throughout society.

Law enforcement officials admit that they intercept only a small portion of the illegal drugs. Their activities only increase the price of the substances and encourage the development of alternative drugs. Some professional athletes have stated that the increased use of cocaine by professional athletes is largely attributable to the crack down on amphetamines.

Experts in the drug area have also said that drugs developed in laboratories from chemicals, such as LSD, have increased dramatically because of law enforcement's focus on the better known street drugs. The great risk to users should be obvious. As law enforcement drives consumers away from well-known drugs with predictable effects, venturesome drug consumers take greater risks with their minds and bodies by trying untested and unpredictable substances.

WHAT IF THE DRUG LAWS WERE REPEALED?

If the laws against drugs were removed, would Americans all become drug addicts and our society go down the drain? There is no reason to think so. This frequently asked question is based on a fallacy; it assumes that people can't currently get illegal drugs. But remember, the current laws do not work. Anyone willing to look at the facts realizes that anyone who wants illegal drugs can get them.

Millions of Americans use alcohol regularly but relatively few are socially impaired by it. After Prohibition was repealed, alcohol consumption did increase, but not significantly, and was not associated with any noticeable increase in alcoholism or other social problems. Eleven states have essentially legalized marijuana for personal use. No one has noticed any significant increase in marijuana use or other social problems in those states as a result. In fact, marijuana use in America has been declining since 1979, before the recent "drug war" hysteria. Americans are also using less legal alcohol and tobacco, as a result of education and social pressure.

What positive consequences might we see from repeal of the drug laws?

1. Organized crime would be deprived of about $80 billion per year in illegal drug profits.

2. The streets and our homes would be far safer because the drug dealers would be gone and their violent turf wars ended.

3. Burglaries, muggings, shoplifting and car theft would plummet as addicts would no longer be paying astronomical prices for their drugs and could support their low cost habits by working at normal jobs.

4. Good kids will be safe from the hotshot street corner drug dealer as role model because he'll be unemployed.

5. Police, courts and jailers could turn their attention to ridding our communities of violent career criminals and billions of law enforcement tax dollars would be saved by leaving peaceful drug users alone. Courts and prisons would no longer be clogged. There would be plenty of room for the real "bad guys".

6. Thousands of peaceful people convicted of illegal drug possession could have their names cleared of the stigma of having been labeled criminals and return to productive lives in society.

7. Illness and death from use of adulterated drugs would plummet as would the transmission of AIDS by intravenous drug users sharing needles.

8. Your right to privacy and your constitutional protection against unreasonable search and seizure by overzealous drug warriors could be restored.

9. People with drug abuse problems would be more willing to ask for help and those who want to help them would have more resources to do so.

10. More harmonious relationships between Americans and people in other countries could develop as U.S. drug warriors end their interventions in drug supplying countries.

CONCLUSION

A libertarian analysis of the drug law issue begins with concern for the rights of the people involved. We must recognize that people have the right to control their own bodies, which means that they have the right to decide for themselves what to eat, drink, breathe, smoke or otherwise ingest. And they have the obligation to take responsibility for the consequences of those decisions.

The second part of the analysis is to examine the practical effects of attempting to suppress peaceful and honest activities. Such laws never work. They do not prevent people from getting what they want. They do cause many unintended, and disastrous, consequences.

If we consider all the negative results of attempting to suppress peaceful activities with criminal laws, and if we compare those results to the positive results to be expected from repeal of such laws, any reasonable person must come to the same conclusion: Just as Prohibition was a disaster, so are criminal laws against drugs, gambling, prostitution, pornography, gun ownership, immigration, or any other kind of peaceful and honest economic activity.

COMPARING LIBERAL, CONSERVATIVE AND LIBERTARIAN

* Should the ownership of firearms be prevented or restricted by law?
Liberal: Yes. No one but law enforcement and the military should be allowed to own guns.
Conservative: Some limitations on hand guns and military "assault rifles" would be appropriate, but not otherwise.
Libertarian: Ownership of a firearm violates no other person's rights, and therefore should not be subject to any criminal penalty or government restriction. It is the aggressive use of firearms that should be punished, not responsible ownership. (See Chapter 15.)
* What should government policy be toward abortion?
Liberal: A woman has the right to an abortion, and if she can't afford it, taxpayers should subsidize her abortion.
Conservative: Abortion is murder and should be subject to appropriate criminal penalties, except, perhaps, in the case of rape or incest.
Libertarian: Under no circumstances should government force anyone to subsidize another's abortion. Many libertarians and the Libertarian Party platform hold that there should be no legal penalties for a woman who decides to terminate her pregnancy. Other libertarians hold that abortion does involve a violation of rights and should be illegal.
* What should government policy be toward nuclear power?
Liberal: Because of high risk and the insoluble problem of nuclear waste disposal, no more nuclear power plants should be built and existing plants should be shut down.
Conservative: Nuclear power is cheap, safe and less polluting than other power sources. Government policy should do more to encourage its development.
Libertarian: Nuclear power is currently a government industry subsidized by legislated limits on liability, not a private industry. Government should get out of the nuclear power business and let private power companies compete in the energy marketplace while bearing full responsibility for actual or potential liability.

For more information see the **Bibliography of Suggested Reading** at the end of the book.

CHAPTER ELEVEN
SOCIAL SECURITY

The U.S. government's Social Security System is in big trouble. During the Carter administration an effort was made to save the Social Security System from collapse by increasing payroll taxes. A few years later, under Reagan, that was found to be insufficient and more changes were made to save Social Security, again by raising payroll taxes. Most workers now pay more Social Security taxes than income tax. But Social Security has not been saved, and most people know it, especially younger Americans.

Today, many older Americans think of the old age benefits under Social Security as the primary source of their retirement. But the system was not designed to serve that purpose.

Unfortunately, the government has put out much misinformation about Social Security, how it works and what it can do. We have been told that Social Security is some sort of insurance, investment or pension plan. People think they have "paid in to" Social Security. This is a mistake. The Social Security system is only a program whereby working people are taxed and the money is immediately paid out to people who are retired. There is no pool of money that anyone "paid in to" which still exists as a retirement or investment fund.

PROBLEMS ARE GETTING WORSE

The Social Security System is insolvent. It should be viewed in the same way as a bankrupt corporation. The system has about $8 trillion in unfunded liabilities. This means that, under current estimates, all of the money which must be paid out in the future — if the system continues unchanged — would equal $8 trillion. The only way to accumulate the money to pay it is to increase taxes on working people in the future.

Right now, more Social Security taxes are being collected than are being paid out because the "baby boom" generation workers are now in their prime productive years. But the government is not accumulating that surplus and investing it for the future; it is gobbled up to reduce the budget deficit caused by other profligate federal spending.

The important point is that our society is growing older. As time goes on there will be more older people, living longer and receiving benefits and fewer younger people working and paying taxes. A person now retiring at age 65 who has worked at average wages for the last 40 years will receive in about two years from Social Security an amount equal to all Social Security taxes he ever paid, about eight years before reaching average life expectancy.

Obviously, that additional eight years of retirement benefits must be paid for by today's working taxpayers. When Social Security began in the 1930s, average life expectancy was about 65, the same age people began receiving benefits. It's great that our parents and grandparents live longer today. But, because they still begin to receive benefits at age 65, the Social Security system is drowning us all in red ink.

Experts estimate that because of the advancing age factor in our population, by the year 2030 the average working person will have to pay over 40% of his or her earnings, just for the Social Security tax, in order to maintain benefit levels as they are now. The system cannot survive under such circumstances.

There will be a major intergenerational conflict. It is increasingly apparent that benefits for the elderly under Social Security and related "entitlement" programs (e.g., medicare) are the largest factor in the explosive growth and cost of the federal government. Younger working people will find ways to evade the system just as many people now work in the "underground economy" to evade excessive taxation. Further, tax increases of the magnitude necessary would be such a depressant on the economy it would cause a complete economic collapse. Thus, rather than providing security, the existing Social Security system is a prescription for disaster and *loss* of security, not only for older people, but for everyone.

A TOUGH SOLUTION FOR A TOUGH PROBLEM

The way to a solution begins by facing up to the hard realities. We must recognize that we are dealing with a bankruptcy situation and the best we can hope for is to end the problem and cut our losses. There is no "fair" way or perfect solution. The following proposal is designed to solve the problem quickly and in the least burdensome way, but does not claim to be perfect. Utopia is not one of the options.

We begin with those people age 56 or older, including those 65 or older already receiving benefits. People in this 56 and older age group would receive 100% of the payout under the proposal. Those in the age group from 51 through 55 will receive a percentage of the proposed payout based on their age: 52 = 20%, 53 = 40% 54 = 60% 55 = 80%.

For each person in the total category (all those age 52 and older) it will be possible to do an actuarial analysis, much as an insurance company would do, to determine the present discounted value of the future Social Security benefits such persons would receive if they lived to the average life expectancy. In simple terms, this would be the amount of money one would need to invest at current interest rates in order to make the Social Security benefit payments to the average person after age 65. This gives us a lump sum figure for each person in the class.

Each such person would choose between taking the lump sum or purchasing a life insurance annuity contract to replace the Social Security benefits they would have received under current benefit schedules. When this is done, the government's Social Security System is ended. There would be no more Social Security tax. All younger workers would be relieved of the increasing Social Security tax burden and the economy would receive a great boost because of the tax relief. An economic collapse and intergenerational conflict would be avoided, and older people would be much more secure than they now are.

Where is the money going to come from to finance this Social Security buyout? We observed above that the system is bankrupt. So is the entire United States government. When dealing with a bankruptcy, the aim is to use the bankrupt's assets in order to pay his creditors at least some percent of what is owed.

The United States government holds a huge amount of assets which are not relevant to its legitimate purposes of national defense and protection of constitutional rights. In fact, the U.S. government owns one third of the lands in the United States. It also owns a multitude of other very valuable assets such as the Tennessee Valley Authority, other power plants, the largest motion picture studios in the world, millions of vehicles, Amtrak, postal service assets, NASA, satellites, etc. Portions of those assets ought to be sold, in a fashion which will maximize the proceeds, to fund the Social Security buyout.

Finally, anyone entitled to receive payment under this proposal who did not actually need it would be encouraged to decline payment.

For more information, see the *Bibliography of Suggested Reading* at the end of the book.

CHAPTER TWELVE

WHAT ABOUT THE POOR PEOPLE?

The federal and state governments manage a large number of programs whereby taxes are extracted from working people and the proceeds of those tax collections, after taking out a sizable portion for bureaucratic overhead, are distributed in a variety of ways to people considered needy and deserving. Social Security is one example, but there are many others: food stamps, aid to families with dependent children, medicare, unemployment insurance payments, etc.

It is true there are millions of people who are poor, temporarily unemployed, disabled or otherwise unable to support themselves. Infants who have lost their parents, the mentally incompetent, very old people and others are unable to support themselves and, therefore, it is indisputable that somehow, someone must and will help them. The question is not *whether*, but *how best*, to help those who need it.

The political issue is: What is the legitimate use of force? Government welfare programs are financed by taxation, a coercive method whereby some people (those in government) use force to carry out the programs they think best by taking the earnings and property of other people. Government welfare programs also cost a great deal of money. It is valuable to compare the results of government programs to the results of the work of thousands of private organizations which also provide assistance to people. That comparison is amazing.

STEP ONE: DECRIMINALIZE WORK

Most people receiving welfare or who are chronically unemployed would prefer to be self supporting rather than in the demeaning position of receiving public assistance. The first thing to do to help the poor is to eliminate all governmental laws, regulations, restrictions, and obstacles to people who would be self supporting if given the opportunity. In other words, decriminalize work.

A perfect example of a counterproductive law is the so called "minimum wage law". Currently, the legal minimum wage is $4.25 per hour. Therefore, it is a crime for two people to agree that one will work for the other at $4.24 an hour or less. This law clearly violates the rights of such people. The effect of the minimum wage law is to make unemployable those whose current job skills are not sufficient to persuade a willing employer to hire them for at least $4.25 an hour. The effect falls most heavily on the inexperienced young people who may be poorly educated in public schools. With no skills or experience it is unlikely that they will find employers to pay them $4.25 per hour, although many potential employers would be willing to take them on at something less as trainees. As trainees, they could acquire work experience at the first rung of the ladder and move up later. But, with the minimum wage law, such youngsters cannot get started in the job market and many of them will be unemployed forever.

Congress is aware of the effects of the minimum wage law and from time to time considers a lower minimum wage for teenagers in order to open up those beginning level jobs. Why doesn't Congress repeal the minimum wage law altogether? Because the hidden purpose of the law is to protect people already working from the competition of younger, newer workers. Since organized labor delivers many more votes than younger, less organized people, Congress will likely continue the minimum wage law even though it clearly causes unemployment among the young and unskilled.

Some people argue that a high minimum wage is required to prevent employers from exploiting the workers by paying them very low wages. This argument ignores the fact that most working people earn much more than the minimum wage. How could that be if employers can grind down the workers to the lowest possible wage?

The answer is that there is a great demand among employers for skilled workers. Because of this competition, workers with skills can demand and receive very good pay, much higher than the legal minimum. The only real effect of the minimum wage law is to cause unemployment among the unskilled and, particularly, the youngest minority job seekers in our society.

LICENSING AND PERMIT OBSTACLES HURT THE POOR

Licensing and permit restrictions prevent many people from going into a variety of occupations. The Interstate Commerce Commission, for instance, for years limited entry into the trucking business, as well as limiting where truckers can ship their goods or what they can carry. This reduces competition among trucking companies and has a serious racist effect, preventing black owned businesses, in particular, from getting started.

The Civil Aeronautics Board provides another example of how regulation hurts and deregulation helps. The airlines were regulated from the beginning by the Civil Aeronautics Board until it was finally phased out in 1985. Until deregulation, not one single new major airline could get started. Since deregulation, scores of new airlines were created, more cities have service and air fares have plummeted. All the new business means more people at work. It is informative that older, established companies invariably want to retain regulatory systems because it protects them from competition, and that smaller, newer, independent companies want to see an end to regulation so that they can offer their services to more people.

Within states, similar regulatory bodies make it difficult for people to start in businesses of various types. Most states limit the number of companies which can offer their services in trucking or moving services. In most cities which are large enough to support taxi service, city governments limit the number of people in the taxi business. The libertarian approach to these situations is simply to eliminate all legal obstacles to anyone offering their goods or services to anyone else. This provides the greatest opportunity for people who are poor or just getting started to offer services that are not now being provided in their communities because of the regulatory obstacles. And, every new small business will put more people to work.

Zoning or other laws which make it a crime for people to work in their homes should be repealed. The City of Houston, the fourth largest city in the United States, does not have zoning. From time to time a proposal is put on the ballot in Houston to allow a vote on whether to institute zoning. Each time the zoning proposition has been voted down. The greatest vote against zoning in Houston always comes from the poorest part of the city, because the people there know that with zoning will come restrictions on their ability to work in their homes and to provide a living for themselves at home.

CUT TAXES AND REGULATIONS

A most effective way to create jobs is to reduce federal taxation and regulation of business. The higher the tax burden, the more difficult for business to open, expand or survive. The same is true for government regulation of business conduct. Surveys of small businesses show that the greatest obstacle for them to expand beyond one or two employees is the additional paper work and government red tape burdens the employer would incur as a result of expanding.

REDUCE FEDERAL SPENDING AND THE DEFICIT

Elimination of the federal budget deficits will also help put people to work. A federal "budget deficit" refers to the difference between the federal government's revenues from taxation and the amount of money it spends in one year. Where does this money come from for this federal government spending in excess of its tax collections? The government borrows money from banks, other lending institutions, and individuals, some in other wealthy countries such as Japan.

The anticipated federal budget deficit for this year is $294 billion and will probably exceed $200 billion per year for the foreseeable future. The Gramm-Rudman law was supposed to result in yearly reductions in the deficit, but Congress and the President can't seem to meet the targets. They invariably come up with some rationalization, like the Savings and Loan bailout or the Persian Gulf crisis, to spend more.

Ten years ago, total federal spending was $591 billion. This year it is about twice that, exceeding $1.1 trillion. Annual budget deficits during the 1970s were generally in the $50 billion range; during the 1980s they ranged from $125 billion to $221 billion. The national debt has tripled in the past ten years and now stands at about $3.2 trillion.

To help understand how this problem feeds on itself, reflect on these facts. Each year's budget deficit is added to the national debt and interest we pay on the national debt currently absorbs more than half the money the government seizes from us in income taxes each year. Coincidentally, the annual interest our taxes pay on the national debt is roughly equal to the current annual budget deficits.

At the current level of budget deficits, about one third of the available financing capital in the marketplace is borrowed by the federal government. The government's borrowing increases demand for money for borrowing, which increases market interest rates — interest being the price people pay for the money they borrow. It also means businesses in the private sector have less available capital for their own purposes. Thus, businesses which would otherwise start up or expand cannot do so. The final result is less employment in the private sector.

A STABLE MONETARY SYSTEM MEANS MORE JOBS

Another factor which causes unemployment is the unstable monetary system caused by the federal government's manipulation of the money supply. The U.S. government controls the monetary system in America through the Treasury and the Federal Reserve System. Because of this, the government can print money, virtually manufacturing it out of thin air. This is what is meant by the term "inflation". The federal government can simply "inflate" the money supply, which it does to pay for projects which the people would be unwilling to pay for through direct taxation on a pay as you go basis. The effect of this inflating of the money supply is to reduce the purchasing power of the money in the pockets of the citizens.

The government's manipulation of the money supply makes the price structure unstable, so that we have volatile inflation rates and interest rates. An unstable monetary system causes unemployment because business operators have difficulty making long range plans in an unstable monetary climate. Business operators shorten their time horizons and do not open businesses or expand them due to the inability to plan rationally. An immediate return to a gold standard for the U.S. dollar would be an important first step toward a stable monetary system. It would encourage people in business to make their business plans on a longer range basis, thus increasing employment opportunities.

Most people not now working could return to productive employment if the government's many interventions in the economy were ended. This would not solve everyone's employment problem, but it would certainly be an improvement. If the people in government would only recognize and respect the rights of all people to offer their goods and services in a peaceful and honest way to others willing to trade with them, then the opportunities for productive employment would increase tremendously for all people.

STEP TWO: PRIVATIZE WELFARE

The second approach to providing assistance for the truly needy is to privatize welfare.

Massive government welfare programs, especially at the federal level, have been with us for the decades. During that time the cost to the taxpayer has increased and the number of people receiving assistance has also increased. A few years ago, economist Walter Williams observed that if all the tax money taken to pay for the government welfare programs were simply divided up among the poor, each family of four would receive approximately $40,000 per year. Obviously, they do not receive it. The question is: who does?

The answer is that the government employees administrating the welfare programs receive most of it. Government welfare is terribly inefficient and certainly does not guarantee that those truly in need are taken care of properly. Many slip through the cracks.

A comparison should be made between government welfare programs and programs of assistance conducted by private organizations such as churches, temples, the United Way, the Salvation Army, the Red Cross, Goodwill Industries, organizations that raise money for medical research, etc. These private groups raise over $100 billion per year in money and services from people willing to support their efforts. They are also much more efficient, their administrative overhead expenditures averaging about 10%.

GOVERNMENT WELFARE HURTS US ALL

Government welfare programs have a number of substantial negative effects. First, the hundreds of billions of dollars per year in tax money taken from working people to pay for government welfare programs is a substantial drain on the economy. If that tax burden were removed, the economy would receive a tremendous boost and many of the people on welfare would be able to go back to work —something the great majority of them would prefer.

Government welfare programs tell the rest of us certain incorrect and insulting things about ourselves. They tell us that we have no compassion, that only legislators and bureaucrats have compassion. They tell us that we do not know how to help people effectively. They tell us that we would be unwilling or unable to provide assistance to the needy unless we were forced to do so.

Government welfare actually interferes with our ability to express and implement our own compassion in our own way for members of our family, people in our communities, and needy people throughout the world. Because of the heavy taxes working people pay, they have little left to use in the ways they think best to help people about whom they are concerned.

Would you stand by and do nothing if your neighbors or people in your community were starving or in some dire need? Of course you wouldn't.

You would help people you see in need. But perhaps you are not so sure *anyone else* would.

Libertarians believe that we must respect the compassion that others have, which is the same as the compassion we experience within ourselves. Most people recognize that government welfare programs are terribly inefficient but still continue to support them, precisely because they do have compassion. People don't want to see others in distress. We all want to live in a world where people do look out for each other when it is necessary.

Government welfare undermines natural human compassion. It induces people to have someone else take care of the problems of assistance. It becomes easier to put grandma in an institution and let others (taxpayers) pay for it, rather than to provide help for grandma in the family home. When it appears that someone else is paying for a service, people tend to overuse that service. But there is no free lunch, and the bill eventually is paid through increased taxes.

Government welfare programs are demeaning. Social workers pry into the personal lives of welfare recipients because taxpayers are naturally and justifiably concerned about welfare fraud, about people who are not "entitled" under the welfare rules to receive assistance.

Combine all this with the natural motivation of welfare workers to perpetuate the system because they are its primary beneficiaries, and we have a situation best described as a "welfare plantation", ever growing and expanding and designed to keep the poor in that condition. Charles Murray's review of the effects of the major federal welfare programs since their beginnings in the 1960s shows that as the programs have grown larger and more costly, more and more people have fallen below the official poverty threshold.

The best thing we can do for the disabled, the needy and deserving is to privatize welfare — to eliminate government welfare programs. The saving in taxes will help the private business sector expand and increase employment. Working people will have more left in their paychecks because of reduced taxes and therefore be better able to contribute to assistance programs of their own choosing.

Some may ask: what will happen to the welfare workers if government welfare ends? These government employees are typically highly skilled and well educated, many with college degrees. Their skills would be in great demand in a rejuvenated economy freed from the crushing welfare tax burden.

With the privatization of welfare, more people will be able to do more, working with others of like mind on real problems of real people in their own communities, so that the most effective assistance can be provided to the truly needy and deserving. This will not create Utopia, of course, but the private way of providing assistance has been proven far superior to inefficient, expensive, demeaning and counterproductive government welfare programs. As a practical matter, personal liberty and responsibility work best.

Nor, can we forget the ever present moral issue. If you see someone you think needs help, you have three basic options. You can do the helping yourself; you can work to persuade others to help; or you can force others to help. To a libertarian, the first two options are morally commendable. The third is morally reprehensible.

CHAPTER THIRTEEN

ECONOMIC FREEDOM: PERSONAL FREEDOM

A libertarian discussion of the economy begins, as always, with a concern for the rights of all persons to do what they desire with their own lives, bodies and property. When people are engaged in business, commercial, or economic activities, they are still human beings. They do not fall into some sort of second class category, with inferior rights, simply because they are engaged in making a living.

People have the right to deal with each other in any peaceful, voluntary and honest manner. This includes producing, selling, buying, and using the great variety of commodities and services available in the market place.

It doesn't matter whether people are Americans or live in other countries, the principle is the same. Production and trade are necessary for people to sustain their lives.

Where the right of all persons to engage in peaceful and honest production and trade is recognized, the resulting economic system is call a "free market". This is a natural state of affairs. As one wag put it: a free market is what happens when no one does anything to prevent it. Libertarians advocate the free market because it is the only system based upon and consistent with individual rights. The free market is also demonstrably the most productive economic system by far, in comparison to any available alternative on this Earth.

Fascism is a political-economic system in which people are allowed to own property but government officials make most of the important decisions about its use, such as wage and price controls, what products may be produced, who is allowed to be in what business, where and how business may be conducted, etc. Although the U.S. is most frequently referred to as capitalistic, or having a market economy, it has clearly had its fascist periods, such as during World War II. Depending on the amount of government intervention and control in economic affairs, a system can cross the line between "market" and "fascist". Many respected observers today say that the situation in the U.S. is more fascist than free market, particularly on the local level with such things as rent control, zoning, growth controls and other limitations on the use of private property.

The political system in which government owns all or most of the major industries is called socialism or communism. Socialist and communist economies also typically allow some private ownership of property such as small farms or shops, but all the significant decisions about resource allocation are made by central planning boards.

LITTLE FREEDOM IN CONTROLLED ECONOMY

Under either a fascist or socialist system, personal and political liberty are much reduced. Individuals have little choice of career, how to use their property best to make a living, or anything else important in the productive areas of their lives. Most significantly, such conditions make it very easy for government officials to stifle any sort of political dissent. Governments which control the ownership and use of computers, printing presses and broadcasting technology, can decide who may and who may not print newspapers, books, or pamphlets. They can control who may and who may not broadcast on the radio and television. Personal liberty depends on economic liberty. Or to think of it from the opposite point of view, the classic communist phrase is: he who does not obey, does not eat.

It is also increasingly clear that democratic political systems depend on economic freedom. People are throwing off communist and other authoritarian governments everywhere. Their common cry is for democracy and market economies. This is no mere coincidence. Control of the economy is the primary tool used by dictatorships to suppress dissent and any challenge to the ruling party elite.

FREE MARKETS MEAN HIGH PRODUCTIVITY

The free market depends upon recognition of people's rights, particularly rights to property. In order to be productive, any person must be able to use the resources which he owns, starting with his own body, in ways he believes will be most beneficial to him. A free market cannot exist or function without legal protection for the right of individuals to own and control their "private property".

The basic reason for the free market's great productivity is that people enter economic transactions on the premise that doing so will benefit them. Two individuals who decide to do business with each other do so because each figures he will be better off as a result. For instance, if I offer to sell you my cow for $1,000 and you decide to buy, this means I have better uses for $1,000 than I do for a cow, and you have better uses for a cow than for $1,000. Each of us feels we can be more productive with what we are getting than with what we are giving up. Each of us will be better off than we were before, according to our own judgment.

Recognizing people's rights and not interfering with their peaceful and honest economic activity increases productivity for everybody. We have an expanding economic pie. People work harder, produce more, save more, are more innovative, when they know they will retain the benefits of their efforts for themselves and their families. This explains why, since the beginning of the industrial revolution in those parts of the world with relatively greater economic freedom, there has been a great increase in productivity and a rising standard of living for all — at the same time that there has been a tremendous increase in population.

Where government interferes least in the economic activities of citizens, economic productivity increases more rapidly than where government controls economic activity. In Hong Kong for instance, the British government intervenes very little in the economic affairs of the people and this small island, with no natural resources, is able to support millions of people.

History provides a laboratory example with East Germany and West Germany. After the devastation of World War II, Germany had to rebuild. East Germany was under communist rule and West Germany was governed by people who followed the advice of free market economists and established a relatively free economic system. The productivity of West Germany since World War II has been viewed as an economic "miracle". The East Germans had no personal liberties and their centrally planned economic system ultimately collapsed, along with many other socialist economies.

Socialism/communism was seen by most intellectuals and many others as the "wave of the future" from the late 19th century until very recently. One of the giants of free market economics, Ludwig Von Mises, in 1922 published his book, entitled *Socialism*, in which he demonstrated why centrally planned economies cannot succeed. Without the pricing mechanism, available only in a market economy, there is no guidance for the planners. There is no way for them to know how to decide how to allocate resources or to know if their decisions were good or bad after the fact. Nor is there the discipline of competition to direct factory managers. Nor is there the incentive of self interest for the workers who receive the same pay whether they work hard or not. Obviously, not much attention was paid to Mises or the other critics of socialism in 1922 or later, until the recent collapse of socialist economies in Eastern Europe and elsewhere finally proved him right.

Today, all socialist economies are finished. Central planning is recognized as hopeless. The big issue in Eastern Europe and the Soviet Union today is how best to convert to market economies. It is gratifying to report that many of the economists there in positions to lead their formerly socialist countries toward the market are looking to the writings of Ludwig von Mises, Friedrich Hayek, and others of their school for guidance. Unfortunately, here in the United States, intellectuals, legislators and policy makers still seem reluctant to end economic intervention in favor of economic freedom for Americans.

REDUCE GOVERNMENT, INCREASE LIBERTY AND PRODUCTIVITY

Every reduction in taxes and every reduction in government control over the economic activity of the citizens will improve America's productivity and increase employment. This would mean an increased standard of living for everybody in the country, and would also mean a much wider variety of choices and opportunities for all persons, of whatever means, to improve their own conditions.

Why do tax reductions improve economic productivity?

When people can enter transactions and negotiate freely regarding the terms of any economic transaction, then all deals consummated improve the conditions of the participants, from their own point of view. Obviously, some decisions and investments don't work out well and some businesses fail. However, when private individuals or companies fail, the loss is their own and others are not obligated to bail them out. By contrast, government can force people to pay for its services and subsidize its losses. It is not subject to a profit and loss statement, nor does it have the incentive of market competition to make it more efficient. When government makes bad decisions, those decisions affect more people and cost much more.

Government waste is a well known phenomenon and is a necessary consequence of bureaucracy, which is not subject to the discipline of the marketplace. This is why, when people in the private sector of the economy are taxed and their wealth is transferred to bureaucrats and then used in a less efficient manner, the economic pie shrinks. Therefore, reducing taxation and the number of government functions will be a net economic benefit, productivity will increase, and more people will be able to find work doing the things which appeal to them most and which give them the greatest opportunity to improve their conditions in accordance with their values. In other words, economic liberty and personal liberty are inseparable.

CHAPTER FOURTEEN
POLLUTION AND ENVIRONMENTAL VALUES

Everyone these days expresses great concern about "pollution" and "the environment". Most have only a hazy grasp of what they are talking about, but the level of concern is quite high. It will help, therefore, to define these terms for purposes of the present discussion.

"Pollution" refers to the act of some person (or company) who removes something he does not want from his property, usually something unhealthy, unpleasant or both, and dumps it on some other property without the consent of the owner of that property.

"Environment" is a confusing term as it is commonly used, because it means "everything out there." It will clarify matters to think of the environment as a combination of all the property in the world, whether owned by individuals, companies or some government. It will become clear that the difference in the way property is treated depends a great deal on whether it is privately owned or is under government ownership.

Environmental issues cover a wide range of concerns, such as: pollution of air or water, wilderness, protection of endangered species or other wildlife, timber or grazing lands, water rights and mining. All of these things have great value to many people. There is dispute, however, over priorities and how best to accommodate them.

THE CHOICE: PRIVATE PROPERTY OR BUREAUCRACY

The choice to be made is between two different legal frameworks. The first is the bureaucratic management model best represented by the federal Environmental Protection Agency, the U.S. Forest Service and the Bureau of Land Management. Most Americans assume that without these agencies our water and air would be fouled hopelessly and private developers would bulldoze the National Parks and replace them with shopping malls and condominiums. The alternative legal framework is based upon traditional Anglo-American concepts of private property under which private citizens can acquire, establish, protect and trade rights in property of all forms. In such a system, government's function is to protect the citizens' property rights, not to regulate their use.

Neither one of these options is perfect. There is no Utopia. But the private property based system, if allowed to work, does a much better job of protecting "environmental values".

Many Americans share certain erroneous assumptions about our present situation and how it works. First, it is assumed that polluters can only be stopped by regulatory officials working for the EPA or similar state agencies. Second, it is assumed that private owners of property have some perverse motivation to destroy its value in the pursuit of short range profits alone. Third, it is assumed that only public spirited bureaucrats can manage forest, grazing lands or wilderness in a manner which does not jeopardize their long term value. Each of these assumptions is false, as we shall see.

POLLUTION IS A TRESPASS

To help understand pollution issues, it is best to start with a simple example. If a person takes his trash to the fence located on the property line and dumps it over the fence into his neighbor's yard, that conduct is clearly a "trespass" and we would all justifiably expect the law to provide a remedy to the victim.

In fact, our law has for centuries provided a couple of very effective remedies. The injured party can sue for an injunction to prevent any further such conduct and can also recover damages for any injury already done to his property. Pollution can and should be analyzed as a matter of common law trespass; that is, one person or company dumping his trash on another's property without consent.

The pollution problems we usually hear about are just somewhat more complex factual situations. Air pollution involves some persons or companies putting airborne trash into the atmosphere which travels to and invades the property of others, including their most fundamental property — their bodies. Water pollution involves some persons or companies dumping trash into water that doesn't belong to them. A major contributor to the problem of water pollution is that the government owns the waterways; private ownership of rivers, lakes and streams no longer exists in America, for all practical purposes. Government has allowed polluters to foul the water, whereas a private owner of water rights in a river would have much greater incentive to bring effective legal action to stop polluters.

Toxic waste is also a problem best analyzed as a trespass. If Toxic chemicals are buried and then travel underground to the property of other persons, the victims should have legal redress against those who did the dumping which resulted in the trespass.

But, having the right to a legal remedy does not always mean the victim will be made whole. Sometimes polluters become "judgment proof" by going bankrupt or just disappearing. This occurs in many situations, not just where toxic wastes are concerned. But if a person's property is damaged by toxic waste, that does not justify having the government force other people to pay — through taxes — to clean up the mess, even where the wrongdoer is judgment proof. The so called federal "Superfund", purportedly designed to pay for toxic waste cleanup, is really a subsidy for companies which have dumped such wastes, for people whose property has been damaged by them, and especially for the companies paid to do the work. Such programs encourage environmental irresponsibility by sending the message that the government will bail you out of your problem. Once again, the average working taxpayer gets stuck with the bill.

POLITICAL BUREAUCRACY IS POOR PROTECTION

Pollution problems are magnified and aggravated by bureaucratic management. Bureaucracy is political. When decisions are made politically, those with the most political clout tend to get their way. Often these are the same people the bureaucracy is supposed to control. After all, if "money is the mother's milk of politics," who is likely to have more money with which to lobby the politicians, big business or the environmentalists?

It should be no surprise that the automobile manufacturers and the United Auto Workers have been able to slow down the development of clean, efficient, non-polluting auto engines. If the courts would recognize the right of private citizens to bring actions against air polluters on the basis of trespass against their bodies and other property, the air would be much cleaner than it is today.

Since the dawn of the *glasnost* era in the Soviet Union and Eastern Europe, the world has learned that the environment has suffered more grievously under socialism than in the more capitalistic West where private property is relatively more respected. Lakes, rivers and the air are so foul in some places in the East Bloc that people are chronically ill and life expectancy is dropping. This should be a lesson to those who urge more centralized government control to "protect" the environment. Central "planning" destroys an economy. It will also destroy the environment, and for the same reasons.

SOVEREIGN IMMUNITY

Another aggravating factor is the principle of "sovereign immunity". This legal principle prevents legal actions by citizens against the government, except where the government consents to be sued. Government owned power plants and sewage treatment plants are some of the worst polluters, but private citizens have no legal redress against them. Respect for private property rights in the legal system and repeal of the doctrine of sovereign immunity would give people the tools to accelerate the job of cleaning up the environment.

BUREAUCRACY CREATES LITIGATION

Some people mistakenly think that replacing the bureaucratic management system with the private property based system would generate a great deal of litigation over environmental issues. The mistake here is to forget that our current bureaucratic system engages the services of hosts of lawyers, both within the agencies and on the staffs of all the regulated companies. Environmental lawsuits are currently a great drain on productivity. By contrast, where property rights are clearly delineated, there is less litigation because potential litigants can more easily determine what is and is not permissible.

PRIVATE RESOURCE MANAGEMENT WORKS
BETTER THAN BUREAUCRACY

The United States government owns approximately one third of the land in this country, most of it in the West and the Southwest. Some of it is Indian reservations, some National parks such as Yellowstone, some forests and grazing lands, some wilderness — and also the outer continental shelf, an underwater shelf off the coast which contains much oil and other mineral wealth. Many environmentalists express great concern that if private owners were to get their hands on any of it, terrible things would happen. But those concerns are largely misplaced. More environmental damage occurs as the result of government management than from private ownership.

As with any bureaucracy, government land managers have no effective way to determine the relative values of different uses, because no market pricing system can develop. People with different ideas about how to use publicly owned resources cannot bid against each other to show which uses are most highly valued. Without the guide of market pricing, the decisions are based on political considerations. So, the people with political clout will probably prevail. If some "strategic material" allegedly necessary for national defense were found in Yellowstone Park, is it likely that the environmentalists could fend off the Pentagon lobbyists? One thing we do know is that the U.S. government loses money every year managing these lands.

The horror stories about overlogging and overgrazing from the past (and present), usually turn out upon examination to be stories of bureaucratic mismanagement. To be sure, private companies would purchase the right to log or graze on government land for a short term and overuse it. But that was the result of agreements that created those very incentives. The government land managers did a poor job of protecting the public trust. Indeed, the U.S. Forest Service often builds logging roads, at taxpayer expense, into national forests to facilitate logging. This is nothing more than a subsidy for logging companies. The Forest Service has also traditionally not required logging companies to pay full price for the trees cut on public land.

By contrast, private owners of forestlands have a strong incentive to replenish the forest crop to maintain the land at its highest value in perpetuity. It is no accident that timber companies like Weyerhauser and Georgia Pacific do a more efficient long term job of using their forestlands than federal and state governments do with theirs. Such efficient use includes not only logging, but the maintenance of game preserves and camping and hiking facilities.

ENVIRONMENTALIST PROPERTY OWNERS

In addition to profit making businesses which own forest-lands, a number of environmental and conservation organizations own forest and wilderness land. The National Audubon Society, for instance, owns 75 wildlife sanctuaries and 100 more are operated by its local chapters. The Rainey Wildlife Sanctuary in Louisiana is a 26,000 acre sanctuary for otter, mink, deer, reptiles and birds. The Audubon Society pays for this operation from royalties from oil and natural gas wells located in the preserve which are operated so as to accommodate the primary values of the preserve and its owners.

The Nature Conservancy is another organization which has seen the value of private ownership for environmental protection. This organization identifies areas of unique value and raises the money to purchase them from voluntary contributions. One purchase was Santa Cruz Island in the Santa Barbara Channel off California. It would probably surprise most people to learn that the major contributors to the Nature Conservancy projects are the very same "big corporations" so many accuse of being environmental destroyers.

Recently we have seen more and more environmental groups coming to the view that private ownership is the best way for them to accomplish their objectives. Keeping in mind that the government operates the lands it owns at a loss, it would be a benefit to the taxpayer if organizations like the Nature Conservancy, Wilderness Society and Sierra Club were allowed to purchase government land having characteristics within their special expertise and concern.

PERVERSE RESULTS OF BUREAUCRATIC MODEL

Our past reliance on government to "protect the environment" has predictably led to perverse results and perpetual conflict. The laws now allow virtually anyone to halt logging, mining, oil recovery, construction of homes, or any other human activity by bringing lawsuits that go on for years. Some environmentalists give the home of a colony of spotted owls a higher priority than the jobs of thousands of loggers and construction workers or the homes which might be built for thousands of families with lumber from trees which can't be cut. Others say humans are a "cancer" on the earth, which would be better off if we did not exist and call for laws to prevent humans from making the slightest change in the "natural" environment. These most radical environmentalists make clear that they believe everything humans have ever done to improve living conditions for humans on this earth has been a disaster and should be undone so all other species, plant and animal, can go on without the blight of homo sapiens to cause them distress. Unfortunately, their emotional appeals frequently impress unthinking government policy makers.

Today it seems that the person who has the least to say about what can be done on any given parcel of private property is the person who owns it. And where government property is concerned, the politicized bureaucratic system ensures a never ending series of conflicts, lawsuits and vigilante violence. There must be a better way.

For anyone concerned about pollution, wilderness, endangered species or other environmental issues, privatization holds much more promise than a continuation of management by bureaucracy. Neither bureaucratic management nor the free market system based on private property rights which are legally protected and exchangeable provides anything like a perfect solution. But the private property framework provides the best available opportunity for the most rational and productive use of all portions of our environment to satisfy the most urgent demands of all the citizens, now and in the future.

CHAPTER FIFTEEN
GUNS, CRIME AND RESPONSIBILITY

All Americans want to be able to walk city streets without fear and to be secure in their homes. In large cities particularly, street crime has increased, as has burglary and armed robbery. Much of this increase is attributable to the "war on drugs" discussed in Chapter 10.

Criminals often use guns as an integral part of their criminal activity. This is true in states and cities where gun ownership has been banned by law or strictly limited. Automatic weapons and so called "assault rifles" are frequently used by criminals, although it is now illegal for private citizens to own them. In most states it is a crime for persons previously convicted of serious crime to own or possess any firearm. Yet, many career criminals continue to obtain guns and use them in the commission of later crimes.

Some people look at these facts and jump to the unwarranted conclusion that guns themselves are the source of the trouble and, further, that depriving private citizens of the right to own any gun at all would end all crime, homicide and injury caused by criminals or negligent gun owners. Some others simply don't like guns, can't understand how anyone could, think gun owners are crazy for wanting to own such nasty things, and will seize on any opportunity to stop gun ownership for everyone — except the government.

THE SECOND AMENDMENT

Fortunately, the U.S. Constitution has something to say on this subject. The Second Amendment states:

A well-regulated militia being necessary to the security of a free State, the right of the people to keep and bear arms shall not be infringed.

There are many reasons why peaceful, law abiding people are concerned that their right to own firearms "not be infringed". To the successful American revolutionaries, one reason was paramount. They demanded a Bill of Rights, which included the Second Amendment, as a condition for ratification of the Constitution. Their concern was to control the new national government, to limit the inevitable tendency of governments to grow and turn into the oppressors of their own citizens. They knew that without firearms, their ability to resist potential future governmental tyranny would be lost. The right to revolt against such tyranny would mean little, without guns in the hands of freedom loving people.

The concern of the American revolutionaries was justified, and is validated by subsequent history. Dictators and authoritarian governments invariably seek to disarm the people to consolidate their power and to deprive the resistance of any hope of success.

BASIC HUMAN RIGHTS

But, there is a reason even more fundamental than the Constitution, to oppose those who would criminalize gun ownership. Individual human rights. The mere ownership of a gun violates no other person's rights. If you own a 357 Magnum pistol, a hunting rifle, a shotgun or a machine gun, I am not harmed by that fact. You may own hundreds of such weapons and the ammunition for them. Doing so does not violate my rights nor the rights of any other person. There is no justification for making you a criminal by reason of that ownership. I must respect your right as a human being, equal to me, to own, possess or use any property of which you are the rightful owner. Period.

It does not matter what your reasons are for wanting to own a firearm: personal protection, hunting, investment, competition shooting, collecting, or because it turns you on sexually. So long as you do no other person harm, no one has the right to complain. Your reasons are solely your business.

Gun control advocates care nothing for either your constitutional rights or your right to control your own life and property. Indeed, they use the term "gun control" to focus attention on the inanimate object and the harm it can do, to disguise the fact that what they really want is to control other human beings, violating their rights in the process.

THE PROHIBITION LESSON

Gun control advocates are much like the prohibitionists of the early 20th century. By making liquor illegal, they spawned organized crime, caused bloody, violent turf wars and corrupted the criminal justice system. We are seeing the same thing today with the "war on drugs". Prohibition didn't stop liquor use; the drug laws can't stop drug use. Making gun ownership illegal will not stop gun ownership.

The primary victim of these misguided efforts will be the honest citizen whose civil rights are trampled as frustrated legislators and police tighten the screws. Banning guns will only make guns more expensive and give organized crime a great opportunity to make profits in a new black market for weapons. Street violence will increase in new turf wars. Criminals will not give up their guns. But many law abiding citizens will, leaving them defenseless against armed bandits.

PERSONAL SECURITY

Americans have the right to decide how best to protect themselves, their families and their property. Millions of Americans have guns in their homes and sleep more comfortably because of it. Studies show that where gun ownership has been made illegal, more residential burglaries are committed. No one has anything to fear from the person who keeps a gun in his or her home for protection, except burglars. The police are simply not able to provide on-the-spot security in your home, your business or the street. They show up after the crime to take reports and do detective work, usually unsuccessfully. The poorer the neighborhood, the riskier it is for residents who seek only to live peacefully and mind their own business. Only an armed citizenry can be present in sufficient numbers to prevent or deter violent crime before it starts, or to reduce its spread. Interviews with convicted felons indicate that fear of the armed citizen significantly deters crime. This makes sense. If a holdup man knows that the clerk and all the other customers in a convenience store just might be armed, he will probably decide the risk to his own health is too great to attempt a robbery.

Statistically, a criminal is more likely to be driven off from a particular crime by an armed victim than to be convicted and imprisoned for it. Thus, widespread gun ownership will make neighborhoods safer.

On infrequent occasions, a psychotic individual will go on a murderous rampage, usually with a gun he has in his possession illegally. The gun controllers typically respond by mounting an immediate effort to pass more laws restricting everyone else's right to own guns. Such an event was the source of the recently imposed ban on "assault rifles". But there are tens of millions of gun owners in America. Of that group, 99.99999% never harm another human being with their guns. Making gun ownership a crime will make criminals out of millions of law abiding Americans who are no threat to anyone. This flies in the face of the traditional American protection for the accused in criminal prosecutions, i.e., to be presumed innocent until proven guilty.

THE DRUG WAR ATTACK ON GUN OWNERSHIP

The "war on drugs" is undermining many of our constitutionally protected civil rights, including the right to keep and bear arms. In the past, Police Chiefs and other law enforcement personnel typically supported private gun ownership. The criminal drug laws have, inevitably, increased violence in the streets among drug dealers fighting over turf. These organized criminals care nothing at all about drug laws or gun laws. They seek out and acquire the most powerful guns, including military hardware. Now, increasing numbers of unthinking police officials are responding by joining the gun control chorus, even to the point of saying only police should have guns, clearly an unconstitutional position.

THE SOLUTION: PERSONAL RESPONSIBILITY

What is the answer? Personal responsibility. Let us recognize that guns are inanimate objects. Only the people who use them can do harm with them. No gun can run amok on its own.

Peaceful and responsible gun ownership and use should not be the subject of any criminal law or legal restriction. Law abiding and responsible citizens do not and should not need to ask anyone's permission or approval to engage in a peaceful activity. Gun ownership by itself, harms no other person and cannot morally justify criminal penalties.

Rather than banning guns, the politicians and the police should encourage responsible gun ownership, as well as education and training in gun safety. We should applaud organizations, such as the National Rifle Association, offering educational programs which teach and promote safe firearm use.

Conversely, the aggressive use of a gun to commit a crime or to threaten other persons, should be subject to severe criminal penalties. And, those who allow harm to come to others because of their negligent use or control of firearms in their possession should also bear the consequences of their negligence under applicable rules of civil liability.

A responsible, well-armed and trained citizenry is the best protection against domestic crime and the threat of foreign invasion. America's founders knew that well. It is still true today.

CONCLUSION

The "libertarian movement" is made up of millions of individuals and an unknown multitude of organizations all sharing a fundamental commitment to certain ethical and political ideas which constitute the foundation for America's great experiment in tolerance and liberty. It is a movement which is respectful of individual differences and values personal responsibility; it values cooperation over coercion; it values independent thought and private decision making; and it values learning from experience to guide the future.

Libertarians believe in the American heritage of liberty, personal responsibility and respect for the rights of others. Those ideas made it possible for Americans to build a society of abundance and opportunity for anyone willing to make the effort. Libertarians recognize the responsibility we all share to preserve this precious heritage for our children and grandchildren.

Libertarians believe that being free and independent is the best way to live. We want a system which encourages all people to choose what they want from life; that lets them live, love, work, play and dream their own way, at their own pace, however they wish and with whom they wish, accepting whatever consequences come.

The libertarian way is a caring, people centered approach to politics. We believe each individual is unique. We want a system which respects the individual and encourages all of us to discover the best within ourselves and actualize our full potential; a system which encourages the development of harmonious relationships among all people.

The libertarian way is a logically consistent approach to politics based on the moral principle of self ownership. All libertarian positions on political issues are consistent with the idea that each individual has the right to control his or her own body, action, speech and property. Accordingly, government's only proper role is to assist individuals when they need to defend themselves from anyone who would violate their rights.

Surely, these libertarian values are shared, in some subtantial measure, by people of good will everywhere.

The libertarian movement, international in scope, is composed of hundreds of organizations and millions of individuals who consciously share and are working to promote these libertarian ideals and values. Hundreds of millions more agree with them, and live their lives accordingly, respecting the rights of others in virtually everything they do. As socialist and other totalitarian governments collapse around the world, the people more and more demand liberty, free markets, and political systems which respect them as sovereign individuals. When given the choice, most people prefer the libertarian way. Not Utopia, just liberty and the opportunity it brings.

In America, and increasingly in other countries, the Libertarian Party is the one organized political party working consistently for everyone's liberty on every issue. It is unique in American politics because it is a party created to promulgate and implement the political philosophy of libertarianism.

In the foregoing chapters we have seen something of the history of the development of libertarianism as a uniquely American political philosophy. Although its roots are in the centuries old natural rights tradition in western culture, it was the American revolution which translated libertarianism into practical political action with magnificent success for the first time in history. The modern libertarian movement is a continuation of that first libertarian revolution.

This book has only scratched the surface of the great body of libertarian analysis and scholarship. It is probable that those who have read this book as their first introduction to libertarianism will have many more questions to ask. That is to be expected. The author is well aware of the fact that most Americans have learned much "history" and "political science" which the contents of this book contradict. For that reason, an extensive bibliography of additional readings on many of the subjects addressed briefly herein has been included for those interested in learning more. Most of the books listed in the *Bibliography of Suggested Reading* can be obtained from the several book sources listed in the *Appendix of Libertarian Oriented Organizations*.

BIBLIOGRAPHY OF SUGGESTED READING

AN INTRODUCTORY SELECTION

The books in this first group are a good place to start for anyone wishing to learn more about how libertarians look at a wide range of issues. They are challenging in the sense that they challenge mainstream political thought, but certainly do not require a graduate degree to understand and enjoy. Most libertarians probably received their first introduction to libertarian thinking from one or more books in this group.

Stephen E. Ambrose, *Rise to Globalism: American Foreign Policy Since 1938* (New York: Penguin Books, 1985)

Frederic Bastiat, *The Law* (Irvington-On-Hudson, NY: Foundation for Economic Education, 1981)

W. Alan Burris, *A Liberty Primer* (Rochester, NY: Society for Individual Liberty, 1983)

David Friedman, *The Machinery of Freedom* (LaSalle, IL: Open Court, 1973, 1978, 1989)

Milton and Rose Friedman, *Free To Choose* (New York: Avon Books, 1979, 1980)

Henry Hazlitt, *Economics In One Lesson* (Westport, Conn: Arlington House, 1946, 1962, 1979)

Rose Wilder Lane, *The Discovery of Freedom* (New York: Laissez Faire Books, 1984)

Robert Poole, Jr., *Cutting Back City Hall* (New York: University Books, 1980)

Ayn Rand, *Atlas Shrugged* (New York: Random House, 1957)

Murray N. Rothbard, *For A New Liberty: The Libertarian Manifesto* (New York: Collier Books, 1973, 1978)

Robert J. Ringer, *Restoring The American Dream* (New York, Fawcett Crest, 1980)

Thomas Szasz, *Ceremonial Chemistry: The Ritual Persecution Of Drugs, Addicts And Pushers* (Holmes Beach, FL: Learning Publications, 1985)

FOREIGN POLICY AND NATIONAL DEFENSE

Raymond Bonner, *Weakness and Deceit: U.S. Policy and El Salvador* (New York: Times Books, 1984)

Ted Galen Carpenter, Ed., *NATO at 40* (Washington, DC: CATO Institute, 1990)

Freeman Dyson, *Weapons and Hope* (New York: Harper & Row, 1984)

David Holloway, *The Soviet Union and the Arms Race* (New Haven: Yale University Press, 1983)

Fred Kaplan, *The Wizards of Armageddon* (New York: Touchstone, 1984)

Jonathon Kwitny, *Endless Enemies: The Making of An Unfriendly World* (New York: Congdon & Weed, Inc., 1984)

Seymour Melman, *The Permanent War Economy* (New York: Touchstone, 1974, 1985)

Robert Poole, Ed., *Defending a Free Society* (Lexington, Mass: D.C. Heath, 1984)

John Prados, *Presidents' Secret Wars* (New York: Quill, 1986)

Earl C. Ravenal, *Defining Defense: The 1985 Military Budget* (Washington, D.C.: CATO Institute, 1984)

ECONOMICS, ECONOMIC HISTORY AND ECONOMIC POLICY

D.T. Armentano, *Antitrust And Monopoly* (New York: John Wiley & Sons, 1982)

Frederic Bastiat, *Economic Sophisms* (Princeton, NJ: Van Nostrand, 1964)

F.A. Hayek, *Denationalization of Money* (London: Institute of Economic Affairs, 1978)

Gabriel Kolko, *The Triumph of Conservatism* (Chicago: University of Chicago Press, 1954)

Don LaVoie, *National Economic Planning: What Is Left* (Cambridge, Mass.: Ballinger Publishing Co., 1985)

Ludwig Von Mises, *Human Action* (New Haven: Yale University Press, 1949, 1963)

Ludwig Von Mises, *Socialism* (New Haven: Yale University Press, 1951, 1959, 1962)

Ludwig Von Mises, *The Anti-Capitalistic Mentality* (Spring Mills, PA: Libertarian Press, Inc., 1956, 1972, 1981)

Alvin Rabushka, *Hong Kong: A Study In Economic Freedom* (Chicago: University of Chicago Press, 1979)

Nathan Rosenberg and L.P. Birdzell, *How The West Grew Rich: Economic Transformation of the Industrial World* (New York: Basic Books, 1984)

Murray N. Rothbard, *America's Great Depression* (Kansas City: Steed & Ward, Inc., 1963, 1972)

Murray N. Rothbard, *Power and Market: Government and the Economy* (Kansas City: Steed, Andrews & McMeel, Inc., 1970, 1979)

Robert Schuettinger and Eamonn Butler, *Forty Centuries of Wage and Price Controls: How Not to Fight Inflation* (Washington, D.C.: Heritage Foundation, 1979)

POLITICAL PHILOSOPHY

Hannah Arendt, *Totalitarianism* (New York: Harcourt, Brace, 1951, 1968)

Hilaire Belloc, *The Servile State* (Indianapolis: Liberty Classics, 1977)

Walter Block, Geoffrey Brennan and Kenneth Elzinga, Eds., *The Morality Of The Market: Religious And Economic Perspectives* (Vancouver, B.C.: The Fraser Institute, 1985)

James M. Buchanan and Gordon Tullock, *The Calculus of Consent* (Ann Arbor, MI: Ann Arbor Paperbacks, 1965)

Friedrich A. Hayek, *The Road To Serfdom* (Chicago: University of Chicago Press, 1944, 1972)

Tibor Machan, Ed., *The Libertarian Reader* (Totowa, NJ:, Rowman & Littlefield, 1982)

William S. Maddox and Stuart A. Lilie, *Beyond Liberal and Conservative* (Washington, DC: CATO Institute, 1984)

William H. Mallock, *A Critical Examination Of Socialism* (New Brunswick: Transaction Publishers, 1908, 1989)

James J. Martin, *Men Against the State* (Colorado Springs: Ralph Myles, 1970)

Charles Murray, *In Pursuit of Happiness And Good Government* (New York: Simon and Schuster, 1988)

Michael Novak, *The Spirit of Democratic Capitalism* (New York: Touchstone, 1982)

Robert Nozick, *Anarchy, State And Utopia* (New York: Basic Books, 1974)

Franz Oppenheimer, *The State* (New York: Free Life Editions, 1914, 1942, 1975)

Murray N. Rothbard, *The Ethics of Liberty* (Atlantic Highlands, NJ: Humanities Press, 1983)

Ayn Rand, Capitalism: *The Unknown Ideal* (New York: Signet, 1987)

Helmut Schoeck, Envy: *A Theory of Social Behavior* (New York: Harcourt, Brace & World, Inc., 1969)

Leo Strauss, *Natural Rights And History* (Chicago: University of Chicago Press, 1950)

Virgil L. Swearingen, *Discovering Self-Government: A Bible Based Study Guide* (Fresno, CA: Advocates for Self-Government, Inc., 1986)

Morris and Linda Tannehill, *The Market for Liberty* (Lansing, MI: Tannehill, 1970)

Henry B. Veatch, *Human Rights: Fact Or Fancy?* (Baton Rouge, Louisiana State University Press, 1985)

SOCIAL POLICY

Doug Bandow, *The Politics of Plunder: Misgovernment In Washington* (New Brunswick, Transaction Publishers, 1990)

Walter Block, *Defending The Undefendable* (New York: Fleet Press, 1976)

W.E. Block and M.A. Walker, Eds., *Discrimination, Affirmative Action and Equal Opportunity* (Vancouver: The Fraser Institute, 1982)

James Bovard, *The Farm Fiasco* (San Francisco, ICS Press, 1989)

CATO Journal, Vol. 3, No. 2, [Symposium on] *Social Security: Continuing Crisis or Real Reform?* (Washington, DC:, The CATO Institute, 1983)

CATO Journal, Vol. 6, No. 1, [Symposium on] *The Transfer Society* (Washington, DC: The CATO Institute, 1986)

Richard A. Epstein, *Takings: Private Property And The Power Of Eminent Domain* (Cambridge: Harvard University Press, 1984)

Peter J. Ferrara, *Social Security: Averting The Crisis* (Washington, DC: CATO Institute, 1982)

John C. Goodman, *The Regulation of Medical Care: Is The Price Too High?* (Washington, CD: CATO Institute, 1980)

M. Bruce Johnson, Ed., *Resolving The Housing Crisis* (San Francisco: Pacific Institute For Public Policy Research, 1984)

Don B. Kates, Jr., Ed., *Firearms And Violence* (San Francisco, Pacific Institute For Public Policy Research, 1984)

Wendy McElroy, Ed., *Freedom, Feminism And The State* (Washington, DC, CATO Institute, 1982)

Charles Murray, *Losing Ground: American Social Policy 1950-1980* (New York: Basic Books, 1984)

Ernest C. Pasour, Jr., *Agriculture And The State* (Oakland, CA: The Independent Institute, 1990)

Ron Paul, *Abortion And Liberty* (Lake Jackson, TX; Foundation for Rational Economics and Education, 1983)

Frances Fox Piven and Richard A. Cloward, *Regulating The Poor: The Functions Of Public Welfare* (New York: Pantheon Books, 1971)

Robert Poole, Ed., *Instead Of Regulation* (Lexington, MA: D.C. Heath, 1982)

Julian L. Simon, *The Economic Consequences of Immigration* (Washington, DC: CATO Institute, 1989)

Julian L. Simon, *Population Matters: People, Resources, Environment and Immigration* (New Brunswick, NJ: Transaction Publishers, 1990)

Julian L. Simon and Herman Kahn, Eds., *The Ultimate Resource* (Princeton: Princeton University Press, 1981)

Thomas Sowell, *Civil Rights: Rhetoric Or Reality* (New York: Wm. Morrow & Co., Inc., 1984)

Thomas Sowell, *The Economics And Politics Of Race* (New York: Wm. Morrow & Co., Inc., 1983)

Thomas Sowell, *Markets And Minorities* (New York: Basic Books, 1981)

Walter E. Williams, The State Against Blacks (New York: McGraw-Hill, 1982)

DRUGS AND DRUG POLICY

David J. Bellis, *Heroin And Politicians* (Westport, CT: Greenwood Press, 1981)

David Boaz, Ed., *The Crisis of Drug Prohibition* (Washington, DC: CATO Institute, 1990)

Edward M. Brecher and Consumer Reports, Ed., *Licit & Illicit Drugs* (Boston, Toronto: Little, Brown, 1972)

Ronald Hamowy, Ed., *Dealing With Drugs* (Lexington, MA: Lexington Books, 1987)

Horace Freeland Judson, *Heroin Addiction In Britain: What Americans Can Learn From The English Experience* (New York: Harcourt Brace Jovanovich, 1974)

Rufus King, *The Drug Hang-Up: America's Fifty-Year Folly* (New York: Viking, 1974)

David F. Musto, *The American Disease: Origins Of Narcotic Control* (New Haven: Yale University Press, 1973)

Larry Sloman, *Reefer Madness: Marijuana In America* (New York: Grove Press, Inc., 1979)

Arnold S. Trebach, *The Heroin Solution* (New Haven: Yale University Press, 1982)

Steven Wisotsky, *Beyond The War On Drugs: Overcoming A Failed Public Policy* (Buffalo, Prometheus Books, 1990)

CIVIL LIBERTIES UNDER ATTACK

Martin Anderson, Ed., *Registration And The Draft* (Hoover Institution; Stanford University, 1982)

Frank Chodorov, *The Income Tax: Root Of All Evil* (New York: Devin-Adair, 1963)

Frank J. Donner, *The Age Of Surveillance* (New York: Vintage Books, 1981)

Morton H. Halperin and Daniel Hoffman, *Freedom vs. National Security* (New York: Chelsea House Publishers, 1977)

George Hansen, *To Harass Our People: The IRS And Government Abuse Of Power* (Washington, DC: Positive Publications, 1984)

David Wise, *The American Police State: The Government Against The People* (New York: Random House, 1976)

EDUCATION AND EDUCATIONAL POLICY

Robert B. Everhart, *The Public School Monopoly* (San Francisco, Pacific Institute for Public Research, 1982)

Ronald and Beatrice Gross, Eds., *Radical School Reform* (New York: Touchstone, 1969)

Myron Lieberman, *Privatization And Educational Choice* (New York: St. Martin's Press, 1989)

Herbert Spencer, *Education: Intellectual, Moral And Physical* (Totowa, NJ: Littlefield, Adams, 1963, 1969)

Joel Spring, *The American School 1642-1985* (New York: Longman, 1986)

Joel Spring, *Education And The Rise Of The Corporate State* (Boston: Beacon Press, 1972)

Joel Spring, *The Sorting Machine: National Educational Policy Since 1945* (New York: David McKay Co., Inc., 1976)

Wm. F. Rickenbacker, Ed., *The Twelve Year Sentence: Radical Views Of Compulsory Education* (La Salk, IL: Open Court, 1973)

LAW AND LEGAL HISTORY

Randy E. Barnett, *The Rights Retained By The People: The History And Meaning Of The Ninth Amendment* (Fairfax, VA: George Mason University Press, 1989)

James A. Dorn and Henry G. Manne, Eds., *Economic Liberties And The Judiciary* (Fairfax, VA: George Mason University Press, 1987)

Henry Mark Holzer, *Sweet Land Of Liberty* (Costa Mesa, CA: Common Sense Press, 1983)

Peter W. Huber, *Liability: The Legal Revolution And Its Consequences* (New York: Basic books, 1988)

Bruno Leoni, *Freedom And The Law* (Los Angeles: Nash Publishing, 1961, 1972)

PSYCHOLOGY

Nathaniel Branden, *Honoring The Self* (Los Angeles, Jeremy P. Tarcher, Inc., 1983)

Peter R. Breggin, *The Psychology Of Freedom* (Buffalo: Prometheus Books, 1980)

David Keirsey and Marilyn Bates, *Please Understand Me: Character And Temperament Types* (Del Mar, CA: Prometheus Nemesis book Co., 1984)

Thomas Szasz, *The Myth Of Psychotherapy* (Syracuse, NY: Syracuse University Press, 1978, 1988)

THE ENVIRONMENT

Terry L. Anderson, Ed., *Water Rights: Scarce Resource Allocation, Bureaucracy And The Environment* (San Francisco: Pacific Institute for Public Policy Research, 1983)

John Baden and Richard L. Stroup, Ed., *Natural Resources: Bureaucratic Myths And Environmental Management* (San Francisco: Pacific Institute for Public Policy Research, 1983)

John Baden and Richard L. Stroup, Ed., *Bureaucracy v. Environment: The Environmental Cost Of Bureaucratic Governance* (Ann Arbor: University of Michigan Press, 1981)

Walter E. Block, Ed., *Economics And The Environment: A Reconciliation* (Vancouver: The Fraser Institute, 1990)

Philip N. Truluck, Ed., *Private Rights And Public Lands* (Washington, DC: Heritage Foundation, 1983)

PERSPECTIVES ON THE WORLD AND PEOPLE

Robert Conquest, *Harvest Of Sorrow: Soviet Collectivization And The Terror Famine* (New York: Oxford University Press, 1986)

Paul Johnson, *Modern Times: The World From The Twenties To The Eighties* (New York: Harper & Row, 1983)

Thomas Sowell, *A Conflict Of Visions: Ideological Origins Of Political Struggles* (New York: William Morrow, 1987)

Alexander Rustow, *Freedom And Domination: A Historical Critique Of Civilization* (Princeton: Princeton University Press, 1980)

AMERICA AND AMERICAN HISTORY

Bernard Bailyn, *The Ideological Origins Of The American Revolution* (Cambridge, Mass.: Belknap Press, 1967)

Frederick Douglass, *My Bondage And My Freedom* (New York, Dover Publications, Inc., 1855, 1969)

Jackson Turner Main, *The Anti-Federalists: Critics Of The Constitution 1781-1788* (New York: W.W. Norton, 1961)

Murray N. Rothbard, *Conceived In Liberty [4 Vols.]* (San Francisco, Cobden Press, 1979)

Louis Ruchames, Ed., *The Abolitionists* (New York: Capricorn Books, 1963)

Thomas Sowell, *Ethnic America* (New York: Basic Books, 1981)

Lysander Spooner, *No Treason: The Constitution Of No Authority* (Colorado Springs: Ralph Miles Publisher, Inc., 1973)

Alexis de Tocqueville, *Democracy In America* (Garden City, NY: Anchor Books, 1969)

APPENDIX OF LIBERTARIAN ORIENTED ORGANIZATIONS

The following organizations are only some of the more prominent and established organizations which have a more or less "libertarian" orientation. Because of the dynamic international growth of the libertarian movement, there are many other organizations which probably ought to be included but for some reason did not make this list. A complete catalog would be larger than this entire book. The author apologizes to all organizations not included and wishes them much success. Readers interested in discovering additional libertarian groups could inquire by checking with any of those listed here.

Adam Smith Institute. 2 Orchard St., London, SWIP 3DQ, England, 01-222 4995; 305 9th St. SE, Washington, DC 20003, (202) 544-8071. Educational and research institute. Publishes studies on privatization, deregulation and free market policy applications.

Advocates For Self-Government, Inc. 940 E. Bremer Ave., Fresno, CA 93728, (209) 441-1776. Educational institute. Organizes local chapters; offers conferences and programs encouraging people to encounter evaluate and embrace the ideas of liberty and improve communications; publishes *Liberator* newsletter.

Atlas Foundation. 220 Montgomery St., Suite 1063, San Francisco, CA 94104, (415) 392-2699. Educational foundation. Educates public on the principle that economic actions have economic consequences; publishes *Highlights* and *Atlas Report*; conducts seminars; provides funding for other free market organizations.

CATO Institute. 224 Second St. SE, Washington, DC 20003, (202) 546-0200. Public policy research foundation; publishes *CATO Journal*, books, monographs and policy analysis material; conducts seminars, conferences and symposia.

Center for Libertarian Studies. P.O. Box 4091, Burlingame, CA 94011, (415) 342-6569. Conducts conferences, seminars and symposia for scholarly business people; publishes *Journal of Libertarian Studies*.

Center for the Study of Economics and Religion. 626 Bute St., Vancouver, B.C., V6E3M1, (604) 688-0221. Promotes dialogue between ecclesiastics with an interest in public policy and economists with concern for ethics and religion; conducts seminars.

Center for the Study of Market Alternatives. P.O. Box 1001, Caldwell, ID, 83606, (208) 454-1984. Research institute. Publishes research on privatization and free market alternatives to government.

Centro de Estudios En Economica y Educacion. 15 deMayo, 1531

PTE, Monterrey N.L., Mexico, 52-83444-824. Educational and research institute. Publishes studies and reports on privatization, deregulation and free market policy applications.

Centro Ricerche Economiche Aplicat. Via F. Crispi 1, 00187, Roma, Italy, 679-3554. Educational and research institute. Publishes studies and reports on privatization, deregulation and free market policy applications.

Citizens for a Sound Economy. 122 C St. NW, Washington, DC 20001, (202) 638-1401. Free market, public interest advocacy group; lobbies for a wide range of free market legislation.

Competitive Enterprise Institute. 2039 New Hampshire Ave. NW, Suite 206, Washington, DC 20009, (202) 547-1010. Free market solutions to environmental problems, antitrust reform and trade; sponsors Jefferson Group pro-market information exchange forum.

Foundation for Rational Economics and Education. P.O. Box 1776, Lake Jackson, TX 77566. Produces seminars, issue papers and books by former Congressman Ron Paul; publishes *Freedom Report*.

Foundation for Research on Economics and the Environment. 7424 Greenville Ave., Suite 114 #20, Dallas, TX 75275, (214) 373-1776. Promotes policy reform supporting conservation and wise use of natural resources based on property rights and market processes.

Fraser Institute. 626 Bute St., Vancouver, B.C. V6E 3M1, (604) 688-0221. Public policy research; Publishes *Fraser Forum* and books and studies on economic effects of government policy.

Freedom Country. Campobello, SC 29322, (803) 472-4111. Kevin Cullinane and staff teach Robert LeFevre's 40 hour "Freedom School" 10 times per year.

Freedom Party of Ontario. Box 2214, Station A, London, Ont., Canada N6A 4E3, (519) 433-8612. Publishes Calendar of Individual Freedom. Publishes newsletters, issue papers; fields candidates for public office.

Free Forum Books. 1800 Market St., San Francisco, CA 94102, (415) 864-0952. Sells wide selection of libertarian books, especially dealing with social issues; store and mail order; publishes books under name of Cobden Press.

Free Market Foundation of Southern Africa. P.O. Box 52713, Saxonwold, South Africa, 2132, 011=642-4407. Educational and research institute. Published studies and reports on privatization, deregulation and free market policy applications.

Free Market Foundation. USSR. 2844 E. Beverly Drive, Tucson, AZ 86716. Educational foundation. Translates and produces libertarian and free market books and materials for distribution within the Soviet Union. Headed by Russian dissident Victor Davidoff. Plans include offices in Moscow and other cities.

Free Press Association. P.O. Box 15548, Columbus, OH 43215. Works to defend and expand First Amendment rights; publishes *Free Press Network* newsletter; sponsors annual Mencken Awards.

Future of Freedom Foundation. P.O. Box 9752, Denver, CO 80209, (303) 777-3588. Educational foundation. Publishes *Freedom Daily*, containing articles on current issues from a libertarian and classical liberal perspective.

Heartland Institute. 59 E. Van Buren, Suite 810, Chicago, IL 60603, (312) 427-3060. Public policy research institute. Publishes privatization and deregulation policy studies and conducts conferences aimed at Midwest editors, news directors and legislative aides.

Independent Institute. 847 Sansome St., San Francisco, CA 94111, (415) 434-2976. Research institute. Sponsors non-political studies on public policy issues; publishes books; sponsors conferences.

Institut Economique de Paris. 35 Ave. McMahon, 75012, Paris, France, 380-1382. Educational and research institute. Publishes studies and reports on privatization, deregulation and free market policy applications.

Institute for Humane Studies. 4400 University drive, Fairfax, VA 22030, (703) 323-1055. Educational institute. Searches for moral arguments and scholarship which support the free society; discovers, encourages and supports scholars in the social sciences.

International Society for Individual Liberty. 1800 Market St., San Francisco, CA 94102, (415) 864-0952. Merger of Libertarian International and Society for Individual Liberty. Promotes international exchange of information and ideas on competitive economic systems with international conferences; promotes campus libertarian organizations; publishes *Freedom Network News* and position papers.

Knowledge Products. P.O. Box 1000340, Nashville, TN 37210, (615) 889-6223. Produces fine audio tapes of great thinkers, many with freedom orientation, e.g., Thomas Jefferson, H.D. Thoreau, etc.

Laissez Faire Books. 942 Howard St., San Francisco, CA 94103, (415) 541-9780. Widest available selection of libertarian, history, philosophy, economic and Randian books, tapes, videotapes; publishes informative monthly book catalog with book reviews.

Libertarian Bookstore. 2086 Yonge St., Toronto, Ontario M4S 2A3, (416) 489-6057. Widest selection of libertarian books in Canada; sponsors seminars and speakers with Citizens for Liberty Forum.

Libertarian Familist. 5205 Fairbanks, Suite 4, El Paso, TX 79924, (915) 755-6940. Family oriented children's rights advocates. Publishes *Libertarian Familist*.

Libertarians for Life. 13424 Hathaway Drive, Wheaton, MD 20906, (310) 460-4141. Supports view that abortion is aggression using libertarian philosophical reasoning rather than religion.

Libertarian Party. 1528 Pennsylvania Ave. SE, Washington, DC 20003, (202) 543-1988 or (800) 682-1776. Political party. Runs candidates for federal, state and local offices; publishes monthly *Libertarian Party News*; holds bi-annual national conventions; issues position papers; information available on state and local Libertarian Party organizations.

Libertarian Party of Canada. 11 Yorkville Ave., Suite 1004, Toronto, Ontario, Canada M4WI13, (416) 323-0020. Political party. Runs candidates for office; conducts annual convention.

Libertarian Press. Spring Mills, PA 16875. (814) 422-8001. Promotes freedom philosophy and the Austrian school of economics by publishing classic works of Austrian economists and new titles.

Liberty Audio and Film Service. 824 Broad St., Richmond, VA 23220. Records libertarian oriented conferences, seminars and symposia; offers wide selection of video and audio tapes; write for catalog.

Liberty Magazine. P.O. Box 1167, Port Townsend, WA 98368. Bimonthly review of libertarian and classical liberal thought culture and politics; contributors include major libertarian movement figures.

Liberty Tree Network. 350 Sansome St., San Francisco, CA 94104, (415) 981-1326. Mail order purveyor of products for life, liberty and prosperity; books, audio and video tapes, games, gifts and collectibles. Free catalog available.

Local Government Center. 2716 Ocean Park Blvd., Suite 1062, Santa Monica, CA 90405, (213) 392-0443. Research center and clearinghouse on privatization; publishes Fiscal Watchdog newsletter; maintains computer database of privatization materials.

Ludwig von Mises Institute. Auburn University, Thach Hall, Auburn, AL 36849, (205) 826-2500 and 851 Burlway, Suite 110, Burlingame, CA 94011, (415) 579-2500. Educational foundation. Promotes principles of Austrian economics; conducts seminars and conferences; publishes books; publishes *Austrian Economics Newsletter, Journal of Austrian Economics* and *The Free Market*.

Manhattan Institute. 131 Spring St., 6th Floor, New York, NY 10012, (212) 219-0773. Educational foundation. Promotes free market with books, symposia and *Manhattan Report* magazine aimed at scholars, government officials and general public.

Mont Pelerin Society. P.O. Box 7031, Alexandria, VA 22307. International association of free market economist and academics. Holds conferences and publishes papers.

National Center for Policy Analysis. 7701 No. Stemmons Fwy., Suite 717, Dallas, TX 75247, (214) 951-0306. Public policy research on privatization with emphasis on health care, welfare and poverty; publishes books, monographs and studies.

National Taxpayers Union. 325 Pennsylvania Ave. SE, Washington, DC 20003, (202) 543-1300. Lobbies for tax reductions; publishes rankings of individual Congresspersons with "Spending Score"; publishes monthly Dollars and Sense newsletter.

Pacific Research Institute for Public Policy. 177 Post St., San Francisco, CA 94108, (415) 989-0883. Sponsors studies and publishes monographs and books with free market solutions to major social, economic and environmental problems.

Political Economy Research Center. 502 So. 19th Ave., Suite 211, Bozeman, MT 59715, (406) 587-9591. Research and educational foundation. Educates in the area of natural resource economics and policy; promoted free market environmentalism; publishes *PERC Reports,* books, law review articles and op-ed pieces.

Reason Foundation. 2716 Ocean Park Blvd., Suite 1062, Santa Monica, CA 90405 (213) 392-0443. Educational foundation. Educates public on principles of free society; Publishes *Reason* magazine; publishes op-ed articles and daily economic education radio program.

Renaissance Book Service. P.O. Box 2451, Riverside, CA 92516, (714) 369-8843. Wide selection of libertarian and free market books; extensive selection in German language; write for catalog.

Services Group. 1815 No. Lynn St., Suite 200, Arlington, VA 22209. Consults on liberalization of economic policies, especially free trade zones, private provision of utilities and education.

WRI Films, World Research, Inc. 11722 Sorrento Valley Road, San Diego, CA 92121, (619) 276-9620. Products and films on economics, inflation, energy, social justice, poverty, and eminent domain with liberty oriented analysis.

NOTES

NOTES

NOTES

NOTES

NOTES

NOTES

NOTES

NOTES

NOTES